I Saw The Smithton Outpouring

(REVIVAL ON A SMALL PLANET)

by
Ron McGatlin

I Saw The Smithton Outpouring

Outpouring
(REVIVAL ON A SMALL PLANET)

Copyright © 2002
Ron McGatlin
all rights reserved

ISBN 0-9654546-5-7

Sermon synopses by Steve Gray are used by permission.

Published by
BASILEIA PUBLISHING
107 W. Independence Blvd.
Mt. Airy, NC 27030

http://www.basileiapublishing.com

Published for

World Revival Church
P.O. Box 9699, Kansas City, MO 64134
http://www.worldrevivalchurch.org
Toll free: (877) 804-5433
Kansas City: (816) 763-0708

Contents

Printed in the United States by:
Morris Publishing
3212 East Highway 30
Kearney, NE 68847
1-800-650-7888

Acknowledgments

I wish to express my sincere thanks and appreciation from the depth of my heart to Steve & Kathy Gray and the wonderful team of warriors and laborers at the Smithton Outpouring for faithfully giving their lives to become stewards of the wonderful outpouring of God and for allowing me and my sweet wife Barbara to be a part. A special thank-you to J. D. King for his years of work compiling historical records and testimonies regarding the Smithton outpouring and for allowing them to be used extensively in this work; also to Randy Lohman for providing quotes and helpful information from his personal Smithton journal. A special thank you to Kim Happs for her work editing this book and for her contribution to portions of the text. Thanks also to Diana Trout for proof reading for accuracy and her helpful suggestions.

***Thank You** to all who have helped and prayed for this move of God which is bringing revival, reformation and the hope of the glory of God to the world.*

Dedication

This work is dedicated to the multitudes of saints of God who have given their lives faithfully over the centuries sowing and cultivating the seeds of revival, while sometimes seeing very little fruit. Without the selfless labor of these faithful ones, we would not be seeing revival in our world today.

IV

Foreword

by

Steven J. Gray

I encouraged Ron McGatlin to write "I Saw The Smithton Outpouring" knowing full well that the entire story of the revival could never be written. Yet, I felt it was important to attempt to capture the essence of the power that came down among us. Most of all, I felt it was important for the next generations to come to be stirred in their souls as they realize what God really did in those days. One book could never contain the thousands of testimonies of lives touched and changed by the power and presence of God, the multitudes of healings, miracles, and glorious manifestations of all that God has done. I believe that Ron, in his descriptive style, has sucessfully captured as well as one book possibly can, the essence of what we saw, felt and heard as the glory of the Lord rained down upon us.

Perhaps the greatest part of the story is yet untold and for the most part shall probably remain so. I speak of the stories of personal sacrifice made by hundreds of faithful people who gave and are yet giving of their time, their money, and their lives to serve God in the Smithton Outpouring. Kathy and I are very grateful to all who have given of themselves to serve with us in this great spiritual adventure. We have been blessed and are very thankful to have the opportunity to give our lives to be a part of this exciting outpouring of God.

Our desire for this book is that it will encourage and inform others who are seeking revival. Although every revival or outpouring of God is unique, there are similarities of receiving and maintaining a sovereign move of God. God is, in this day, sending forth

His Spirit bringing revival fire to spots of our world. When the fire comes upon a church or group, God expects and looks for a response from His people. When the people respond by laying aside other agendas and programs to make Christ and His work of revival the center of their lives and continue to do so, the outpouring continues and the visitation of God becomes a habitation of His presence. Our total desperation at the time of the fire fall in Smithton had prepared us to properly respond to the outpouring by emptying our calendars and focusing our lives on Him. Through the years we have diligently sought to maintain this level of desperately seeking Jesus and His kingdom.

Mat 6:33: But seek ye first the kingdom of God, and his righteousness; and all these things shall be added unto you.

Stephen J. Gray
Senior Pastor, World Revival Church
Kansas City, Missouri
(Formerly, The Smithton Outpouring)

Preface

The story of this book is very unfinished and must remain so. Though others will update it from one season of God to the next, it cannot be finished as long as time and mankind remain. This is also one of the most inadequate books ever written. My feeble attempt to capture even a small particle of the mighty works of God in this outpouring borders on utter foolishness. The magnitude of the powerful works of God, the sheer glory of His purity and holiness can never be captured, chronicled, or described. All the books in the world cannot contain the scope of His mighty works. The most eloquent words of earthly language cannot describe His glory. The more I know him — the more I see His marvelous works — the more inadequate and unworthy I am to even attempt to describe His perfect, pure and holy works. Truly there is no god like our God.

I am blessed among men to have been able to have lived long enough to have seen the beginning of the time for which many great men of God labored, prayed, longed, and died yet did not see except from a distance. Despite all its glory, this revival has only just begun.

Though there are mighty men and women of God pouring out their lives for world revival, there are no big name stars. Only humble, dedicated, miracle-working men and women filled with the power and love of of Jesus. The absolute purity of the Lamb of God indwelling the people of God by the Holy Spirit clears the way for the full power of God and the pure revelation of truth to come forth into our world.

The Smithton Outpouring is a part of the revival touching our world, and it was, in its beginning, a forerunner of the purity of God, bringing power on earth to transform lives and reform the church. The dead religion of the past is becoming compost for the reality of the kingdom of God to rule and reign, bringing forth the glorious church that our Savior is building.

CHAPTER 1

Fire Fell From Heaven

The congregation of Smithton Community Church had gathered for evening services in the tiny Missouri farm town of Smithton, Missouri. An air of uncertainty hung over the people who for two weeks had been led by the pastor's wife, Kathy Gray. Pastor Steve Gray had left town, a broken man in search of more of God for his own life. The stress of bitter criticism and rejection by some who had been close friends had added to his disappointment and frustration of preaching, teaching, and praying for revival for over twelve years. He had done all he could do, and there had been a good measure of success. The Smithton Community Church was a healthy congregation that filled the church building. Yet, year after year for twelve years Pastor Steve Gray had told his flock, which had grown from about a dozen people to around 180, that revival was coming to the local church. He taught about revival and sought to prepare the people for it, yet corporate revival had not come to the church.

Their church had a lot of life, and the praise and worship was good. Everything was good. They believed the presence of God was there, but there was a problem. It seemed to some of the people that they would move right to the gate, only inches away, but could not enter into revival. It was like an invisible wall existed, and just before entering all the way into an awesome outpouring of God, they were stopped and could go no further.

Yes, there had been a lot of life coming forth, and some of the people felt they were experiencing personal revival within themselves and their families. The last walls that could be removed from the sanctuary had been knocked out to make room for the people. The first time new people came to the church, they were usually impressed with the spiritual life and anointing in the people. But corporate revival and the great outpouring of God by His Spirit was always just out of reach beyond the invisible wall. Sincerity and commitment in the church was strong. Perhaps it was a lingering residue of past religious training and experience, which allowed a little stiffness to set up an invisible barrier to revival. Pastor Steve was loved and respected by the congregation, but he was in the natural sense a rather shy person. His desire to do things properly in church may have contributed to the stiffness that hindered the revival that he had desperately sought for years.

THE VALLEY OF DARKNESS

In the fall of 1995 things began to happen that set the stage for a journey through a valley of darkness and brokenness. Unseen by those involved, God began to bring together those who were to be a part of the miracle fire fall. Tom and Diana Trout, Steve's sister and her husband, were forced to leave Antioch on October 15, 1995. The congregation they had loved and served rejected them. A few weeks later Mike and Nancy Thomason, Steve's other sister and her husband, left the Open Bible Fellowship in Neosho, Missouri. Both couples, saddened and in despair as a result of their circumstances, began attending Smithton Community Church.

The church at this time was thriving, active and powerful. With the strong preaching and great music, the church had become a powerful force in the kingdom of God. Yet a struggle had begun within Steve. Even though the church had grown from 13 to 180 people over twelve years in a town of only 532 people, he began to wonder if he had missed a higher calling.

He later said about this time, "Years went by, and I started to wear out mainly because of dealing with people. For many years I had preached that revival would come to America; I became empty and desperate in my own quest for God. We had many good moments but not many God moments. I had taught them everything that I knew how to teach them. What is there left? I was so tired of giving out information about God."

"So after twelve years I began to hear things in the world...revivals, little fires springing up. Yet, it was not happening in my place. I began to feel a little stuck in this small town. Where am I going? What am I going to do? After years of sitting, hoping and dreaming, you start moving in the other direction. You start thinking, 'This is not going to happen.'"

"Then as things progressed, my sister came to me one day and she said, 'I have got a word from the Lord for you.' And it scared me. Really scared me. I didn't like what I heard; I didn't even want to think about it. But when it came true, it was painful and hurtful."

Diana later spoke about this word. "The Lord came to me with a warning for my brother. It was really a difficult time for me because I was a little fearful in telling him about it. But the Lord was so specific to me saying that, 'Steve would be betrayed by some people that he cared deeply for.' And I felt that if I didn't warn him, I would regret it for the rest of my life. So I went to him and told him that he needed to be prepared for this."

Pastor Steve's trusted close friends who were leaders in the church turned against him and had subversively sought to entice people to leave with them. Steve later said, "Suddenly some people changed, they became very mean. To me it was almost as though you were sitting across the room dipping your bread in the sop and Satan entered their heart for absolutely no reason. There was not a fight, no division. We didn't have a disagreement. It wasn't like we had a split. Nothing! Nothing happened, and suddenly they were different. I was the same. It broke my heart. My heart just collapsed. The life went out of me."

Chapter 1
Fire Fell From Heaven

Steve's desperation had reached such a point that he considered giving up the ministry and just leaving everything including his family. A part of him just wanted to empty out his bank account and run away, far away, perhaps to a remote island where no one would know him. On Sunday morning, March 10,1996, he preached a sermon on the woman with the issue of blood and how she had spent all she had and yet was none better. He thought this might be his last sermon. He had given all he had to make the perfect church and to bring revival, and he felt things were none better. He had not accomplished that goal, and now he had spent all and was empty. After he finished preaching the sermon, he left town in search of something, mostly a way to get out. Steve later had this to say about this moment, "As I walked down from that pulpit, I had reached the end. I didn't know what the future held, but I knew that I couldn't really go on anymore. Whether I left the country, left the church, or even left the ministry, one thing was certain...I couldn't continue what I was doing in my present condition. Something had to change." Kathy and Steve decided that he would go to the Brownsville Revival in Pensacola, Florida to have a reasonable excuse to tell the congregation for his leaving. Steve later said, "I had been at Smithton for twelve years and had spent all I had, and I was still no better. So I preached the sermon and left. I drove away hopelessly. I didn't even know why I was going there. I just knew I had to find Jesus again. I was not after revival. I was after survival." This total brokenness was exactly that for which God was waiting so He could make major changes in Pastor Steve Gray and his congregation. The betrayal by close friends and the subversive attack that followed was used to prepare Steve for the breakthrough of a lifetime. Breaking through the invisible wall of limitation would open the way for the powerful outpouring of God to come, and it set the Grays and the Smithton Community Church on a course of revival destiny to touch the world.

I Saw The Smithton Outpouring
(Revival On A Small Planet)

Since Pastor Steve had left two weeks previously, the congregation was going through some soul searching. They were crying out to God for answers to their questions of uncertainty and apprehension. It was a day of darkness bordering on despair. If God had brought revival in other places in other times and was sending revival in some places in this time, why would He not send revival to our thriving but hungry congregation of Smithton Community Church? Getting his first glimpse of hope, Pastor Steve had called Kathy from Pensacola, Florida and told her that he had been in the best church service he had ever experienced in his life. Kathy repeated this in the service, expecting it to encourage the people, but this bit of news had just the opposite effect. One of the elders of the church came to the microphone at the Tuesday night prayer meeting on March 19, 1996 and said, "If we don't have the true presence and power of the Lord, then we might as well shut this place down. We cannot go on without the Spirit of God. Why would our pastor have to travel a thousand miles and go to a different church to experience the best service that he has ever been to?" The tears flowed as the men of the church came to the alter and cried out to God on their faces, "God what is wrong with us? Why does revival come to others and not us? Why are we shamed that our Pastor must go somewhere else to find revival? God help us!"

One of the elders of the church speaking of this time, later said, "I was broken and severely devastated. It was darkness. It was a time of night. It was nighttime for us, so to hear about churches dancing before the Lord? It sounded so wonderful, but it was still nighttime for us. Weeping was still enduring, and I can remember how our men were just lying on the floor, crying. We didn't know why we were crying; we just knew that it was night. And when you've wept all night, bitter weeping over bitter moments, over crushed times, you've done it seemingly over a lifetime. Our whole life was gone — I mean dead. We were covered with a thick blanket of death. There was no life. There was no movement of God. Imagine hearing about things — that your pastor had been in the best church service of his life, and there's still the cover of darkness over you and your church. You hear of joyful jumping, rejoicing in the camp, but there's still a cover of darkness over your life and over your church."

THE LIGHT OF EXPECTANCY DRAWS NEAR

Wednesday night March 20, 1996, the children began to prophesy to the congregation. Some spoke of God's goodness and grace; a few began to say things about his holiness. Finally, a little 5-year-old girl climbed out of her father's arms, pointed her little finger to the sky and began to proclaim to the congregation. **"It's coming, it's coming! I know it's coming!"**

Sunday morning, March 24, 1996, was the last service before the fire of God came. There were expectations that something was happening, but no one was really sure just what or just when. Kathy finished a series of messages on "The Holy Spirit of Promise". In this particular sermon, she emphasized the subject of joy by the power of the Holy Spirit. Kathy encouraged the people that they should be praising God full out and dancing before Him with great joy. They should lift themselves up and worship Him with all they have until they break through their darkness into the life and presence of God.

Reflecting on that time Kathy later said, "Steve called me on the car phone. It was raining. He said, 'I'm coming. I'm coming, and I don't know what is going to happen tonight. I don't know if God is going to break through. I don't know what is going to happen, but my life is in God's hands.'"

No one could have known how much everything was about to change. God had been working on the congregation in Smithton while He had been working on Pastor Steve Gray in Pensacola. Both Steve and the congregation had experienced deep changes of brokenness and a readiness to accept, without limitations, whatever God would pour out from heaven. Kathy Gray had been ministering powerfully to the congregation, challenging them to press into the Lord with praise and dance. At the same time, Steve was watching the powerful praise, worship, and dancing before the Lord in Pensacola. The people were in place, and everything was set, like a stack of kindling soaked in gasoline just waiting for a spark to ignite it.

THE FIRE FELL

The spark of ignition came on the evening of March 24, 1996. The congregation had begun praising and worshiping with strength and excitement, seeking to break through the darkness. Kathy repeatedly checked her watch as she anticipated the return of her husband. He had called and said he was on the way home. Some of the people were gathered at the front of the church praising the Lord with singing and dancing. For the first time in his life, Eric Nuzum had been helping with praise and worship during Steve's absence. Tonight he was again leading praise and worship as the congregation sang, "Who is like the Lord?" At 6:12 PM, Kathy glanced at her watch as the door next to the platform opened and Steven J. Gray started walking toward her to give her a hug. Suddenly, as he was walking toward her their whole world changed in an instant. A bolt of spiritual life and power struck Steve like lightening from heaven. He began to jump and shout and twirl, literally supercharged with the life of God. Quickly the entire congregation rushed to the front and was ignited with the same power, and nothing has ever been the same

Chapter 1
Fire Fell From Heaven

Later Steve described the event, "It was raining as I drew close to town. I pulled my car into the same parking place in which I had parked for 12 years. I walked into the same door and heard the sounds of worship coming through the walls. I pushed open the sanctuary door, saw Kathy on the front row, and decided to give her a hug. She was just grinning at me. I took about eight steps toward Kathy to hug her, and wham! Like lightening, the Lord hit me. My arms shot up in the air, the weights lifted, and I began to jump up and down. It was not a planned response; it was the only response."

Kathy Gray reflecting on the moment said, "Steve glowed with life. And he began jumping and twirling and praising God. He had never jumped in church before."

Eric Nuzum changed the song when Steve walked in and began playing and singing, "Shouts of Joy" a fast song with significant words of joy and victory for the righteous of the Lord. He later said, "I can remember looking over there and actually seeing him jump and twirl. I thought in my mind, 'Something is happening here' I had never seen him do anything like this. Even in my inexperience, I knew I had to change songs to capture this new moment in time that was standing before us. After the first couple of bars of 'Shouts of Joy', everyone ran forward."

One young lady, reflecting on the moment ,said, "Eric had been helping with worship while Steve was gone. When Steve walked in, Eric quickly yelled out, 'Switch songs,' and twirled his hand around in the air. We began singing, 'Shouts of Joy". One of the only fast songs we really had. We all raced up to the front, shoes were flying everywhere as people began jumping and dancing. Never in my life had I seen such a sight. I looked at pastor. He was just standing there with this look of shock on his face. Then he started — well jumping and twirling around with this silly grin on his face. I had never seen him look so happy."

15

Steve later said, "Suddenly we were different. We were having the best time, and totally confused, I tried to speak. Though my mind was clear, my mouth wouldn't work. God's joy was pouring in and out of us."

Though the presence of God was so thick that Pastor Steve could hardly talk, he began to speak his heart. His words were slow and slurred and his speech interspersed with crying. In tears, he said he didn't deserve for God to visit in such a powerful way. He spoke of the force of hunger. "Blessed are those who hunger and thirst for what is right. That is the short form of it. And revival is right, healing is right. Sickness is wrong; bondage is wrong, fear is wrong. So we hunger to bring back to the earth and to our neighborhood what's right. You hunger for that. Hunger is a powerful force; it's a motivator. Hunger will make you a beggar. Hunger will make you a fighter. Hunger has caused wars, and hunger causes revival. It's hunger that causes revival. God's promise to hungry people is, 'You will be filled.' Why? Because you are hungry." He went on to tell them that he believed the greatest revival the world had ever seen is out there now. A much greater revival than what he had seen in Pensacola. He spoke of revival no longer being just "up there" but now being right here. "We just have to reach out and pull it in." He spoke of it not being a matter of praying it down any longer, but that it was just a matter of pulling it in because it's right out there now.

The prayer ministry part of the service was very different. Pastor Steve began to pray for people, and the new powerful presence of God was apparent. People began to be struck by God with many falling down, which was not a normal occurrence in services before that night. Many wept, and at the same time, there was a lot of joy. People embraced each other with sincere emotion of the love of God, even the men were holding each other, and a deep sense of unity moved into the group.

Chapter 1
Fire Fell From Heaven

One of the church elders later spoke of the prayer ministry time, "The prayer time ensued and Steve began to pray for the people. Some fell to the ground, which had not really happened in a service at Smithton Community Church. Many were struck by God as they sought after Him. I remember quite a few falling down, a lot of joy, and a lot of crying. Most of all I remember no one wanted to leave, and everyone's hearts opened to each other. There were people lying in each other's arms crying and stroking faces. The guys were even hanging on to each other. The congregation was unified. Oh there were some on the fringes, but most were hit with a great sense of unity."

Steve said regarding the prayer time, "I offered to pray for people. Although I didn't lay hands on anyone, people I had known for years started collapsing and crying. I was awestruck. When we finally ended the service late that evening. I said, 'I don't really know what to do, but I'm going to come back tomorrow night and pray. If you want to come, you can.'"

On this day, the prayers of years had given birth to a move of God destined to touch the world with fresh life and revival fire leading toward reformation. Neither Pastor Steve, nor Kathy, nor anyone else really knew that the small church in Smithton, Missouri USA was to eventually touch churches across this nation and the world. Neither did they know what to do or what to expect next. And surely no one had a glimpse of where all of this would take them in the years to come. Yet everyone knew that, for the first time, they felt fully alive and more excited than ever. They had finally broken through the invisible wall. It was as if they had all been supercharged with energy from heaven as they were plunged into the heavenly fire of God.

An elder again speaking about this moment, later said, "Imagine at one swift moment for the hand of God to come down and say, 'The night is over.' The light of day comes and reaches down and takes that blanket of darkness, and all of a sudden, the glorious light of God stands before us. Let me tell you about a day that changed our lives, when the light blinded us, when it was so bright that we didn't even know what it was. We had been so dark! We could hardly comprehend what we were or what we were supposed to be, or even Who He was, but light came and pulled us out of darkness. So the weeping ended, and the joy came in the morning. Let me tell you about a day of life and rescue, a day of salvation, a day of change."

Daniel Gray, reflecting on that evening and the glorious events that followed, said, "God blew the doors off the little church and drowned the membership's traditional Charismatic mind-set in the river of power and energy. Before anyone could figure out what was going on, the church was literally jumping! Not just a figure of speech! The whole congregation was jumping up and down to the powerful praise that had burst forth. Eventually people were collapsing to the floor as if cut down by some awesome Holy Ghost machine gun. I remember my whole family was there, sisters, brothers-in-law, nieces, nephews and kids moving together in a river. New kinds of prayers, new terminology, 'More Lord, More Lord' — 'Fire of God fall now, now, now!' It was very powerful!"

Pastor Steve Gray said to the people at the close of the service, "I am going to come back to church tomorrow night and pray and seek God to try to discern what is happening and what to do next." The next night the whole congregation showed up to pray and seek God with him. The same fire was there, and the same excitement was upon and within the group as the night before. They worshiped and praised God with new fervor. Everyone wanted to be back at church each of the following nights just to again experience the wonderful presence of God that came upon them every time they came together and began to worship Him.

No one called it a revival and no schedule of meetings were set at that time. There was just so much life that people wanted to be together in the presence of God every night. Powerful things began to happen, and people from other churches began to hear that something was going on and began to show up at the nightly meetings.

Apparently, Pastor Steve Gray and the congregation had become so desperate for God that He had heard from heaven and sent a mighty outpouring of His Spirit that continues today and is touching the world. No one had any plans to build anything or to start a worldwide movement. Mostly they saw themselves as the least of the least and were desperately seeking to just get up to zero. They merely wanted to get back up to normal from the pit of despair, insignificance, and uselessness in which they saw themselves. This was truly a movement of innocence and dependence upon God. If they could have seen the importance and timeliness of this move that was to touch the world and bring reformation to the church, they would have probably fainted away or perhaps sought a place to hide.

WHY SMITHTON?

Pastor Steve later said that he believed that for a moment in time he became the most needy, the most desperate man on the face of the earth, and God had pity and decided to respond to his desperation. He also has said the he believes many others were on God's list to receive this outpouring ahead of Smithton, probably many greater churches in larger cities. But for some reason, they were not able to respond and receive it, and finally somewhere on down the list Smithton was chosen to receive and care for this mighty outpouring of the Spirit of God. Pastor Steve also said, "Thank God that even though we were not at the head of the list, at least we were on the list."

Many pastors and leaders hunger for the fire of God to be poured out upon them and their congregation. They may long to know God's miracle working, life changing power in a mighty outpouring of His Spirit upon and within themselves and their people. Some have prayed for two or three years, maybe even longer, for a mighty revival to fall from heaven upon their church. They may even have become rather desperate for a move of God. Some have indeed experienced powerful moves of God with miracles and angelic visitations as the fire of God poured out upon them in response to their desperate prayers and longing for Him. Yet after a season, the fire leaves, and the people often descend to about the same lifestyle they lived before the outpouring came. Those people among them who desire to remain in the fire of God will often move on to somewhere else where more spiritual life is being demonstrated. So what is the difference? Why has the fire of God continued, for over five years and counting, to pour out through Steve & Kathy Gray and the other humble servants? Why has He continued to move through this mighty army of broken men and women who are mostly of low esteem in the eyes of the world and virtual nobodies in the social and political religious circles?

As Pat Robertson once said to Steve Gray regarding the Outpouring of God in the small church in the tiny town of Smithton, "You have taken away all of our excuses for not having a revival." Through the experience of Smithton, we now know beyond any doubt that it can be done and that God is willing and ready to pour out His Spirit anywhere to spark a world-touching revival movement

Pastor Steve says the main reason people pray for an outpouring of God in their church and don't receive it is that they are not really as desperate as they think they are. They are not yet willing to make room in their lives for a move of God. They want God to come and make their church better, make their lives better, make their people better, but they are not willing to give up their lifestyles and allow God to do as He pleases. They are not willing to give up some of their religious doctrines and methods, their golf and TV, or their sports and hobbies to make room in their lives for a move of God. God does not send revival to bless our plans and make the things we want to do better. Revival will totally change the way we live, the way we think, and the way we do church. Deep in their hearts and minds, most are not yet really ready for such radical change.

The reason an outpouring comes and remains only for a season is basically the same. The people have come to a level of desperation and cried out to God until revival comes. Sometimes it is the pastor or leadership of the church that is crying out to God for an outpouring and the congregation is slow to follow, but at other times it is people in the congregation crying out to God for revival and the pastor or leadership is dragging behind. When both the leadership and the people come together in seeking an outpouring from God, and make room in their lives for a move of God, it will come. The reason it does not remain permanently is that the people or the leadership begins to be concerned again about the things of this life. Pressures and desires for natural things begin to rob them of the room in their lives for the move of God, and it will not continue.

The church in general, through the years, has seen moves of God come and go, so many people have come to believe that it is the plan of God for there to be hot spots and seasons of revivals and spiritual outpourings and for those to then fade away. It is not God's plan for our fervor and His presence to fade away due to our declining interest and unwillingness to make room in our lives and churches for the move of God to continue. Indeed, there are phases of revelation and restoration that cause an exciting emphasis on the freshly returned gift or manifestation for a season. That exciting emphasis will fade as further gifts and works are restored; yet they remain in the church. It is God's plan that we move on with each new piece of revelation and continue forever to walk in His presence, in His Spirit. It is His plan that we continue to bring His kingdom of heaven ways into the earth. Revival is changing our world into a reflection of the kingdom of God in heaven on earth, the way God designed it to be.

When Steve Gray became so personally desperate that he was no longer seeking to better himself and his church, when he could no longer come up with a plan to fix things, when he really no longer had a life and a desire for a church or a ministry, then there became room in his life for the move of God. The revival for which he and others had prayed and prepared over twelve years now had a place to reside. At that point, he literally had nothing else better to do. Revival will not come and will not stay if we have anything else better to do. Only when we have emptied our calendar, emptied our lives and become an empty vessel can we experience the outpouring of God. And if we begin to have other things to do, we will not continue in the outpouring of God. Even good ministry things may prevent an outpouring of the Spirit bringing revival in our lives.

When my wife, Barbara, and I were considering moving to Smithton, and later to Kansas City, to give our lives in revival, God spoke clearly in my spirit and asked me a question. He asked me if I would give up teaching the kingdom for revival. This shocked me because it is my life message and is powerful revelation given to me by God in an awesome way. Then He went on to explain to me that revival could only come in us if it was our entire focus. He showed me that the outpouring of God in Smithton is bringing revival, which is bringing the kingdom lifestyle into the church and world. He said, "Revival brings kingdom, teaching kingdom does not bring revival." God again redefined my life and created a single focus upon Him and His awesome presence bringing revival to the church and then to the world.

It does not matter how wonderful our gifting, or ministry, or service for God really are, or how sure we are God gave them to us. If it is more important to us than an outpouring of God and His powerful presence bringing revival, we will not be in the front line of His revival fire. This does not mean that other ministries are not important or that they should not continue and are not of God. It only means that there is not enough room in life for two or more equal focuses. Seeking His kingdom and His righteousness means seeking Him and His life within us. It means coming into total obedience to His desires and His ways of living and being. This causes us to be effective in doing whatever job He has for us at the time.

YOU GIVE THEM SOMETHING TO EAT

When the disciples came to Jesus and suggested He send the thousands of hungry followers away from that desert place in order to buy bread to eat, Jesus did not say, "Wait a moment, and I will call down manna from heaven for them." He said, "You give them something to eat". After having the disciples bring the people together in order, He then took the little that they had, the loaves and fishes, blessed it, and gave it to the disciples to feed the thousands. The days of manna falling from heaven are passed. God now will take what little we have bless it, multiply it, and have us feed the thousands with it. Revival is not going to fall from the sky without our willing participation. He is going to take the little of those who are truly following Him, those who are not hanging onto their natural life and old ways, and use it to bring revival. He will use us to bring the people together in order and bring the spiritual bread of real revival to them. They will be miraculously fed bringing strength and fresh life by our hand, not as manna from heaven without our participation. However, we will not be with Jesus feeding the thousands if we are busy minding the store, or maintaining our church programs, or clinging to other things. The disciples left their nets, or their tax booth, or whatever and followed Him, and in doing so, they became a part of the great outpouring of the first century.

We are again experiencing a great outpouring similar to the first century, only greater in scope and magnitude. Steve and Kathy Gray, along with hundreds of people of the Smithton Outpouring, have altered their homes, jobs, and businesses to make room in their lives for the move of God. They have become a people of His presence, who have a part in bringing revival and reformation to the church and the world. That, in part, is why the revival continues and is increasing at World Revival Church in Kansas City USA.

The first years of the outpouring after the fire fell were like no other in the history of the Smithton Community Church. Nothing was the same as it had been before revival struck. Powerful new life permeated everything about the small church. The electrifying flow of power from God changed everyone present and began to flow out to churches across the nation and around the world. A sense of destiny was an ever-present atmosphere surrounding the Smithton Outpouring. A destiny from God, worthy of the sacrifice of the things of this life, led the people forward and kept them going as weeks became years of living in the fire of God.

CHAPTER 2

Before The Fire Fell

The original church building where the fire fell and the Smithton Outpouring began was built in 1859-60 in Farmer City, Missouri about 5 miles west of Smithton between Smithton and Sedalia. Followers of Bart Stone and Alexander Campbell in the fervor of the Cain Ridge revival days built it. A number of people had come from Kentucky to Farmer City and became part of a reformation movement. It was a reformation toward practical matters and simple unity while much of the church in America was debating baptism style and other doctrines. They said, "Where the Bible speaks we speak, where the Bible is silent we are silent."

The railroad was planned to go through Farmer City and a depot was to be built there. For some reason the railroad paused in Smithton and eventually the decision was made to make the depot in Smithton and not in Farmer City. When the railroad built depots in Smithton and Sedalia but missed Farmer City it became a ghost town. Farmer City dried up and most of the people attending the church there went to Sedalia. The remnant of remaining people decided to move the church building to Smithton in 1873. The building was cut into quarters and loaded on ox carts and moved to Smithton and put back together on the site where it remained and served the people of Smithton for over a hundred years.

In 1980 the building was closed and the doors padlocked for lack of interest. The building then sat vacant for four years. The people who had been the church leadership had left or passed away. In 1984, there remained one trustee alive in the area who had the keys and the deed to the old church building and property. He had for years kept the yard mowed and generally looked after the place,

25

but he was coming to the point where he could no longer continue to take care of it. For more than a century, the church had been kept in good repair, including updates like the addition of bathrooms onto the back of the building, but it had become rundown and disheveled without proper maintenance. The local people wanted to see it torn down and the property put to some other use. A granddaughter of the last remaining trustee did not want to see the old building torn down, but no pastor could be found who would restart the old church. No pastor was interested in coming to such a small town where there were other active churches and the people obviously had little interest in the old dead church.

In January of 1979, Steve and Kathy Gray had moved to Smithton from Sedalia. They moved there because it was a small quiet town where they could relax between trips with their traveling ministry. They had a group called Jubilation Ministries and were traveling and ministering in music and Word. Steve's family is quite musically talented; most of them have music degrees. The Holy Spirit had swept through the family in 1974-75, and they were all baptized in the Holy Spirit. They started singing together on weekends, and by September 1977, they had grown into a national full-time ministry. Jeanne Gray, Steve's mother, spoke for the group in the very early days. However, it was not long before Steve began preaching the Word.

Jeanne had a profound spiritual influence in her children's lives, helping to lead them into the baptism in the Holy Spirit. She was a Methodist who began attending a Spirit-filled type prayer group where she was baptized in the Holy Spirit and fell desperately in love with Jesus. Jack Gray, Jeanne Gray's husband and father of the children, had passed away at an early age. The emptiness in Jeanne Gray's life from the loss of her husband was filled with loving Jesus.

The members of the group were Steve and Kathy Gray, Steve's mother, Jeanne Gray, Steve's two sisters and their husbands, Tom and Diana Trout, Mike and Nancy Thomason and Steve's brother Daniel Gray. It is interesting to note that the entire family group that traveled as Jubilation Ministries, except Jeanne Gray, was back together in Smithton at the time of the outpouring and each person is still heavily involved in revival. Jeanne Gray had passed away about five years before the outpouring.

Steve began to write the songs for the group. Their "Promises" album was widely popular across the U.S. The song "Promises," and others from that album, were in the top ten on several Christian radio station charts. They sang and Steve preached in hundreds of churches across the U.S. for almost seven years. The group was climbing the "gospel ladder of success," appearing on The 700 Club, Toronto's 100 Huntley Street, other Christian radio and television programs, and many large "Jesus Festivals."

While on one of the road trips in 1983, God spoke to Steve to stop the traveling ministry and make a change. He told Steve, "Revival is coming to the local churches in America. The people of God will no longer be touched and changed in the large convention halls, but at their own church altars." They promptly canceled future engagements and returned home to Smithton, seeking God and looking for what He wanted them to do next.

For a season Steve served as associate pastor of a church where the pastor was supportive of them as they sought the Lord for their future and waited on His timing. As the Grays spent time in the community and became more acquainted with people, they were repeatedly asked to take the old church building in Smithton and restart the church, and they continued to respectfully decline.

"I WOULD RAISE THE DEAD."

About that time, the Grays received a very good job offer that seemed tailor-made for them. It was a job as associate pastors at a good solid church near Chicago. The pastor was looking forward to retirement in a few years and wanted to train Steve as his replacement. It was a solid position in a solid church, offering all the job benefits the Grays could imagine, and the church was not considering anyone else for the position.

In the midst of all the excitement of this great offer, people continued asking them to reopen the little dead church in Smithton. Finally, to appease those asking, Steve said he would pray about it; fully intending to finish packing and get moving toward the new job in Illinois. Steve is a man of his word, and since he had said he would pray, he asked God what He wanted to do about the situation. He knelt in the living room floor and told God about all the wonderful advantages of the new job in Illinois and reminded God about the dead, run-down church that interested almost no one. He then asked, "Jesus, what would you do?" Instantly, he was overwhelmed with the clear, unmistakable answer, " I will tell you what I would do. I would raise the dead." That surely was not the answer Steve was expecting nor what he wished at the time, but it was the beginning of the Smithton Community Church that eventually brought the great Smithton Outpouring that is touching the world.

THE FIRST SERVICES

A musty smell greeted Steve as the door creaked open the first time. The old church had dark paneling, red carpet, a cross on the front wall with light bulbs in it, and old pews that had been stained so many times they were black. Dust and dead bugs covered the sanctuary, and the whole thing smelled of dead mice.

After some clean up and fix up, it was time for the first service. Steve put a freshly painted sign in the yard that read, "Church Tonight". On Thursday night, April 19, 1984 the first service of Smithton Community Church was held at the little church at the intersection of Clay and Chestnut streets in Smithton, Missouri. A total of thirteen people were present for that first meeting. The old building in the tiny town that didn't even have a gas station or a coke machine was again filled with the sounds of worship as it had been since 1860.

Danny Gray had called Steve before he decided to re-start the church and told him that the Lord had directed him to help Steve in his next ministry venture. Dan later said, "In early 1984, I felt that the Lord directed me to help my brother, Steve, in his next ministry endeavor, although I had no idea what that would be. I called him and told him what I felt the Lord had said to me. It wasn't long after that conversation that my brother told me he would soon be re-opening the little church in Smithton. I thought he was off his rocker, but I was obedient to the vow that I had made to the Lord."

There were two Thursday night services in April, and the people who came wanted to have Sunday services. On the first Sunday in May 1984, the first morning service was held. Some of the people who had attended the former Christian Church attended the service and sat on one side of the church while the Grays and other "charismatic" members sat on the other side. When Steve and Danny began to play "We Bring The Sacrifice of Praise" and other charismatic choruses, one side of the church was clapping and smiling and the other side sat with blank, astonished looks on their faces. It was their only time to visit the new church.

People started to come to the services where the young preacher was bringing a revolutionary message of reality in seeking God and really living the Word. Steve began from the beginning boldly proclaiming, to mostly empty pews, "Revival is coming!" Steve was preaching to the heavens and preached as though he was speaking to thousands. He would stand before the congregation and read vivid accounts of the Welsh Revival and the Great Awakening. He would describe the phenomena and the crowds — the prayer and the people. He caused the people to feel what revival would be like. A message began to emerge that revival was not just for saving the lost but changing the lukewarm church. Steve's desire was to build a church that God wanted to attend. Practical biblical teaching and powerful messages began to build a congregation of strong families with increasing spiritual maturity and commitment.

Steve was lifting up a higher standard that caused some people with less commitment to drop out from time to time, but others coming in with a higher level of commitment usually quickly replaced them. The higher standard and quest for holiness was interpreted by some other charismatic groups in the area as pride and a "holier than thou attitude." Steve actually expected the members of his congregation to live and walk in the spiritual and natural provision of the Spirit and the Word. This was a revolutionary message to the lukewarm, half-hearted religious system. Churches in the area were often filled with sleepy Christians who believed they had their ticket to heaven when they died and not much else mattered, but it was a powerful, life-building and overcoming message for the people of the Smithton Community Church. The sound Biblical teaching, centered on commitment and the overcoming Christian life, built faith in the people. The promise of coming revival built hope in their hearts. The spirited praise and worship brought sincere joy in the presence of God. The little congregation grew in strength and in numbers, from 13 to around 180 over the next twelve years, before the fire fell on March 24, 1996 and the Smithton Outpouring began.

CHAPTER 3

The First Years of Outpouring

The first years after the fire fell were filled with awe and great joy for the congregation that was experiencing God in a way they had not known before. There was an innocence and naivete about the group who had never before seen miracles and powerful manifestations like the ones that began to occur among them. They were sometimes a bit afraid when some new powerful thing began to happen to someone in the congregation.

In the first weeks of the revival, the most profound change was within the individual people. God was preparing them to become people of His presence and to give the revival fire and freedom it produces to others. The Spirit brought supernatural transformation within the people. Hardness of heart was broken away. Religious traditions were torn down. Man-made limitations were removed. Fears were dissolved and lingering impurities washed away. The wind of God blew in and quickly began to blow all these things away. The same wind also blew in the greatest thing — the thing that had to be in place before the revival could begin to change others — an awesome level of pure devotion to Christ, greater devotion than they had ever known. This deep devotion led to increased loyalty, commitment, and faithfulness to God and to one another.

The years of foundational teaching of the Word had prepared the people for the mighty work of the Holy Spirit coming in like a great wind and bringing life to their hearts. Kathy Gray once said, "It was like wind and fire, a hurricane and an explosion, and life just burst into our church." One of the members who had been at Smithton for many years said, "Steve had paid the price for revival up front. I believe that it was the foundational teaching that got us to where we are. It, along with other things, opened the door to revival."

THE FIRST DAYS OF OUTPOURING

In the first week of the revival, the changing power of the Holy Spirit became evident. Pastor Steve along with others was being dramatically changed in the presence of God. Hearts were melting and being reformed. The entire congregation came back on Monday evening after the fire fell Sunday evening. They continued coming every night of the week and then would start all over again on Sunday.

A young girl had this to say about the second night of the revival. "The following night, which I believe was Monday, the lights were dim. I remember walking through the door and seeing my pastor, laying flat on the floor with tears streaming down his face. This was the first time that I had ever seen him like that. I realized at that moment that this was more than just jumping around and shouting. This was deep and very serious. Pastor was not the only one on his face. There were many others who were doing exactly the same thing. Some were praying quietly while others were shouting at the top of their lungs. All of this was new. Pastor Steve later told us that he would be there the next evening and everyone came again."

The whole church kept coming back every evening with growing expectations, and the awesome presence of God was there every time they came together. On Wednesday, the fourth night of the revival, Kathy Gray got up and said, "I believe this, my friends, is the prelude to something great, something big. This is the rumbling of revival."

Another young lady later spoke of her hard heart being changed during these days. "When revival started and I saw others receiving, I was like, 'How am I supposed to receive, because my heart is so hard and I have so much sin and stuff I have built up?' I would try to receive, and my head would start to spin. I could never get anything into my heart. Everything about Jesus was all in my head, and there was no love in my heart. He would say, 'Just receive!' Part of me didn't want it, and another part was craving and crying out, not able to get it. I was so far away, and I couldn't get any closer. I needed a miracle. I needed Him to come and break through the hardness. If He didn't do it, I was going to die. After awhile, the desperation of not being able to receive started to build up inside. I got a real desperation, and my heart started to break. I was so sick of being hard. It took a few weeks, but the hardness started to crack and break. Finally, I didn't care what my mind or other people thought about what the power of God was doing to my body. I just wanted God to break through, and I started repenting and crying out for Him to break through that hardness. My mind shut down, I started to receive, and 'lightening' started to get in my heart. Fire started to get to my heart. All of the sins I had been living with, the hardness, the resistance and rebellion started to leave, and life came in."

The people were being rapidly changed to minister to the outsiders who would begin to come at week three. Prior to week three, Pastor Steve could hardly speak. He was being changed, and a new revival message was being planted within him. He had been a leader and a teacher, but now he was being transformed into a revivalist preacher. Steve later said, "During the first weeks, I was literally speechless. I could hardly talk. The few sermons I had were very short, but I think God was developing the revival message within me because I really did not have a revival message." As

Steve's voice was returned to him, he began to preach powerful revival messages, and spontaneous altar calls began to occur as people under great conviction would suddenly break forth like a stampede running and throwing themselves on the altar.

Tim Dieckmann later talked about Pastor Steve's powerful preaching of that time. "It wasn't what he was saying, it was how he said it. You could look into his eyes and be transformed. Most of what he was saying was not all that profound, but his look of amazement gripped us. It was the amazement in his eyes that gripped us. I can't get over how much crying and grief transpired. It was a time when everyone became aware of where they were in the Lord. I think that this was a time where the Lord had to deal with the simple things that we needed to get rid of in order to do what we needed to do in the future. It's funny there wasn't much said. The Lord was confronting us there. When something was said, it was potent and challenging. I don't think anybody had an idea about a 'big revival'. We just knew that we needed more of God. Up to this point it seemed that God was dealing just with us. Things changed when visitors began coming. God placed people in front of us who were in the same condition that we had been in. He wanted us to help bring freedom to the people just as He had brought freedom to us."

Dramatic miracles began taking place immediately as the explosive power of God was released among the people. The people felt that Jesus was right there with them in a tangible presence. Some described it as the presence of God was in your face, you could talk to Jesus, and He would answer you back instantly. Phenomenal, supernatural things began happening in the first few weeks.

One church elder speaks of one of the early incidents that impressed him at week three of the revival. "It was shocking! I saw this lady sitting there rubbing her head. I asked her if she felt bad, and she related she had had a severe migraine headache for three days and that it was really bad. I just said, 'Please touch her Lord,' just the usual kind of prayer. In about twenty minutes, I looked over there, and she obviously was still not feeling well. I said within myself, 'Oh — why not? Why didn't anything happen?' Then I just cried out loud, "JESUS, Jesus." And instantly, He said, 'What?' He was right there just like He was standing next to me, but it was nose to nose. I began to gasp and couldn't speak, like 'uhh wha uhhh ughuhh hungh huuh'. The feeling I had was like I had just got caught talking about someone as they walked into the room. I was mealy mouthed like 'aba duhh dah bah abah ahh. What are you doing here!?' I recovered a bit and said, 'I'm going to pray for her in your name, OK?' And He said, 'OK'. That was it. I didn't touch her, and I was three or four feet from her when I spoke, ' In Jesus' name'. That's all I got out when, WHAM! It was like somebody dropped a hand grenade between us. She went flying backward against a wall and slid down the wall and lay there. I fell up into the pews. It was like someone went BOOM and hit me right in the middle of the chest, and I flew backwards. Here I am lying there in the pew belly laughing and saying, 'Wow! What was that!?' I got up and saw that she was out in the Spirit, and much later when she eventually got up the headache was gone. This is the kind of thing that was different, this in your face tangible reality of the presence of God, and this sort of thing was happening all over the place. People's lives were getting changed instantly. People were not only being knocked several feet across the room by the power of God, but there were also dramatic fallings. It was like their legs were suddenly cut out from under them, and we had no catchers. We didn't know anything about catchers in those days."

Pastor Steve began telling the people there was now an open heaven over them and encouraging them to go out and invite people, the sick, the addicts, those in marital stress. He told them that the things they had tried in the years before that would not work, would work now because the heavens were open above them.

One of the elder's wife remembers inviting their neighbor. She was fatally ill with some kind of blood disease and was being treated at Mayo Clinic. Doctors had said she had three months to live. She said, "Our next door neighbor was dying. She looked like death, emaciated, bad color, just about gone. She and her husband came at week three. They were both filled with the Spirit, and she was healed. She is yet alive to this day. They came back only one more time about week 15, but she is healed and alive to this day almost five years later.

Some described the powerful presence like standing under a tornado of fire just over your head, sometimes feeling weightlessness like your feet were lifting off the ground and then suddenly being thrust several feet away across the room. Powerful prophecy would come forth literally changing people instantly. Prophetic praying began to come forth.

There was a major concern and fear in those early days that the fire might go away. Everyone was terrified that it might go away. Much care was taken to try very hard to do everything to assure the fire would not leave and to do nothing that might cause God to pull away His glorious fire of revival. If visitors were not worshiping God during the worship time, they would be spoken to and encouraged from the platform. If they did not respond to this, someone would come to them and tell them how important it was to honor God and for everyone present to worship Him together. They would stand there and press the people into worship so that the power of all might prevail and God be honored.

Chapter 3
The First Years of Outpouring

THE PEOPLE START COMING

A group of Methodist started coming around week 3, 4, and 5, and the flow of people coming from other churches began. Soon the building was filled to capacity, and by week 11, the move was made into the church gym, which had been converted into a revival hall. The gym was about three quarters filled, and corporate prayer changed as they began to cry out to the East and the West and the North and the South for the people to come. In the next service, the building was filled as the stream of people from across the nation and around the world began arriving at the tiny Smithton Community Church where the outpouring of the Spirit of God was changing lives.

Richard Roberts heard of the outpouring from other ministers and invited Steve and Kathy to be on his "Something Good Today" show. The next weekend, large numbers of people began to arrive. One man wrote in his journal, "The revival broke open this week. There was deep, deep conviction and humbling repentance that took place. On Friday the floodgates of people flew open. We had the largest crowd to date. There were no seats left in the auditorium (gym). People were coming from all over the nation. We saw demonized, tormented people set free every service. There was usually some strong shaking and falling down with some shrieks and some strong convulsions. However, when the people got up, they were happy, bright and fully recovered. The people of our congregation are the ones who were praying. The pastor directed us toward who to pray for."

The same man also said, "We were facing demons every service. I recall praying for this lady I had never seen previously. I was pushing demons off of her and this huge thing appeared behind her and stood behind her threatening me. We learned early that once you engaged the demons in combat you could not disengage or back up. The powers of darkness would quickly take over and begin showing themselves if you did not continue to forcefully attack them and drive them away. If you slacked off for a moment they would aggressively take over the situation. We became tenacious prayer warriors."

People began to rise up to fill needs in every situation. God raised up strategic people in strategic positions of service from within the congregation, and over time began to bring people in to fill other strategic positions of service. People who had never before done things became prayer leaders, prayer warriors, intercessors, musicians, singers, sound technicians, audio/video people, greeters, car parkers, ushers, worship leaders, security people, office workers. Management in every area, from housekeeping to publications and conference coordinating, all grew into place like grass growing in a field. In many cases, the people were supernaturally equipped to do what they had never done. Some who had never played musical instruments began to play. God's grace was poured out with His Spirit to meet the needs of the two hundred and fifty thousand people who would eventually come through the doors at the converted gym/revival hall in the sleepy town of Smithton.

REVIVAL MUSIC BEGINS TO COME

Music began to flow from God through the praise and worship team. **Eric Nuzum** wrote worship songs while driving his forklift that have now been heard and played around the world. Music has its distinct sound in every move of God. The Smithton Outpouring is no exception. The same joy and excitement of a people set free and moving in revival that caused people to jump and shout flowed through the powerful original music of the Smithton Outpouring. In addition to other CDs, an original music CD of the Smithton Outpouring was recorded by Integrity Hosanna and released in August 1999, called, "The Smithton Outpouring - Revival From the Heartland". The early music at Smithton was very fast and filled with fire and great rejoicing as it boldly proclaimed, "This is revival", with songs written by Smithton Outpouring worship leader, Eric Nuzum. Including songs like, "Revival is in the Land", "Spirit of Revival", "Refiners Fire", "Outpouring Power", "Still Small Voice", "God is on the Move", "The Rain Will Fall", "In the Current", "I've Got the Peace", "You Have Called Me", "Fire in the House" and more. Eric Nuzum also co-wrote "Prepare the Way" with Darrel Evans and "Healing Waters" and "More of You Lord" with Chris Springer.

In talking about one of the major changes brought by the revival, Kathy Gray often says, "My husband got his song back." **Steve Gray's** song writing took on a vast dimension of reflecting the intensity of the hunger of the people and the devotion and commitment of those making the journey into the freedom of revival at Smithton. Pastor Steve Gray wrote moving songs such as: "Pour Down From the Skies", "Return to the Lord", "God's got a Good Thing Going", "I'm Back in My Father's House", "Trial of Your Faith", "One More Time", "When Heaven Came Down", "I Want To Tell You I Love You", "Shine Your Light", and "Living Sacrifices". One very touching song, entitled "Burning Ships Upon the Shore", is frequently requested because it is so characteristic of the attitude of commitment of the Smithton Outpouring. It speaks of an army leaving themselves no possibility of retreat by burning the ships in which they came to the battle.

Daniel Gray wrote powerful songs in a guitar blues style that reflected the world's condition and told deep truths of the changes brought by revival. Danny's songs were sometimes humorous and always challenging. Songs like "The Whole World's Got The Blues", "Let The Power Flow", "A Generation Walking", "Glorious Church", "Christians Just Like You", "Take A Look At You", "Come To Me Now", and "You're Not Following Me" continue to impact many churches and individuals.

POWERFUL MANIFESTATIONS COME

Manifestations became prevalent, powerful, and at times frightening to the unpretentious people of Smithton who had never seen such things before they actually began happening to them. One very proper lady was one of the first people in the early days of revival to begin violently shaking as the power of God surged through her body. Soon she and others would begin shaking, vibrating, or falling to the floor and continue doing so for a long time. Pastor Steve would look on and say something like, "I don't know what is happening, but I know this person." The shaking would sometimes continue for days and in some cases even weeks. Often people were unable to leave under their own power and would have to be carried out at night. Accompanying the weeping of repentance, mixed with sincere rejoicing and feelings of euphoria from being set free, there were many such powerful manifestations, and Pastor Steve was not excluded.

One of the elders spoke of an occasion in the early days when Pastor Steve was "jolted" by the power of God. "People responded during the worship time, and the front of the building was full, from the platform to the first row and up the aisles about three quarters of the way to the back of the auditorium. The presence of God was so mighty that I fell down three times; I guess I should have stayed down. Then Pastor Steve stepped down and touched a couple of guys. Then he got 'jolted' from the platform all the way into the front row. He left in his wake about fifteen people who were on either side of the path he traveled to the first row. People from nine to sixty years old, teens and middle aged, all went down by the power of God."

In those first days, people would fall at times as if their legs had been cut out from under them and then sometimes lay as if frozen for long periods of time as God dealt with them internally or supernaturally changed them. Some would freeze in position standing up and were unable to move or change position without someone assisting them. Tim Dieckmann became frozen in place while standing during pre-service prayer. Eventually he just fell over like a stiff tree. One of the elders said that on one occasion in those first days he was on his knees up front, crying uncontrollably before God. His crying became wailing with deep burst of snorting type sound on the in breath and wailing on the out breath. He said he began to realize he sounded a lot like a donkey braying. Within himself he called out to God. "God what are you doing to me? You're making me sound like a donkey braying." He heard the heartbreaking reply, "Why not? You are stiff-necked and stubborn like a donkey."

REPORTERS AND CAMERAS COME

By March of 1997, the word was getting around about the phenomenal outpouring in the tiny town of Smithton, Missouri USA, and the reporters and cameramen began to come from the internationally known Christian media organizations. In April 1997, the 700 Club broadcast a story on revival that included a major section on the Smithton Outpouring. Charisma printed an article on the Smithton Outpouring in the May 1997 issue of Charisma Magazine. Charisma Magazine returned several times and published several more articles on the Smithton Outpouring over the next few years. Newsweek magazine even came to the outpouring in April of 1998 and did an article called "Living In The Holy Spirit". Christianity Today magazine published an article on the Smithton revival in April 1998 called "The Cornfield Revival". Magazines as far away as Singapore and Germany printed articles about the outpouring. Steve & Kathy appeared on major Christian Television programs numerous times. Several interviews were aired on CBN, including one, which might have been the longest personal interview ever on the network. Several scheduled segments were canceled to continue the interview with the Grays. Steve and Kathy told the story of the Smithton Outpouring numerous times on the Richard Roberts show and the Lindsey Roberts Womens show. They also appeared on Sid Roth's program, "Something Supernatural". Warren Marcus independently produced a 90 minute documentary video in 1998. This powerful reenactment video has continued to impact the world with the story of Steve and Kathy and their journey into revival. Hundreds of churches around the nation and the world were directly impacted as the first Pastor's Conference was held in Smithton in September of 1998. Steve Gray's first major book "When The Kingdom Comes" was published by Chosen Books and released in 1999.

THE REVIVAL MOVES OUT TO OTHER CHURCHES

Even with the great activity of so much that God was doing, Steve & Kathy began a traveling ministry carrying the revival to churches across the world early in the revival. Often a number of faithful people from the outpouring would travel with them and help with ministry. By April of 1998, Steve had made three ministry trips to Israel and from San Antonio, Texas to New York and Washington, DC the fire of revival had begun to be spread.

Through International Pastors Conferences, Steve Gray captured the hearts of pastors with explosive meetings as each night the attendance increased as people come from many different cities and across national borders to gather at one central location. Never wavering, Steve preached the same message of pure devotion, loyalty, commitment, sacrifice, eliminating the competition for Jesus in your life, dying to self and living for Him. He said, "In the New Testament, the Kingdom of God breaks in, and the four gospels are an account of what people did when the Kingdom arrived. What are you going to do with it? Will you adjust your whole life to it?"

Pastors and leaders from over fifty nations of the world have come to the Smithton Outpouring, and invitations have poured into the office for Steve and Kathy to speak across this nation and the world. A powerful ministry has developed to the world through Steve and Kathy as they travel and carry the anointing of the Smithton Outpouring. Even with all the traveling, they almost never miss one of the regular Outpouring Services at home.

THE REVIVAL MESSAGE COMES

In the early days of the outpouring, Pastor Steve and others assumed that the message and ministry of this revival would be like earlier revivals. The great revival in Argentina emphasized supernatural, power evangelism and deliverance. The powerful message of the Toronto revival had been largely the love of the Father and the Father's blessing, restoring the reality that God loves you as an individual and wants to meet with you in a personal powerful way. God's presence came forth in corporate meetings bringing great healings of body, soul, and spirit along with powerful manifestations. The message of the great Brownsville revival in Pensacola had been repentance and giving your life to God. Lost sinners, drug addicts, prostitutes, and people of all ages, but especially youth entangled in the sins of the world and living in gross darkness, were drawn to the meetings. Literally hundreds of thousands rushed to the altars to repent over the years. But equally as powerful in Pensacola was the message of repentance to preachers and Christians who were battling the same darkness in their personal lives as the lost sinners. It was not uncommon to see pastors and lost sinners rushing together to the altars to repent and be cleansed of sin at any of the meetings.

The pivotal momentous message of the Smithton Outpouring began to be formed in the early days and became more clearly defined in the first years. The message and ministry of the Smithton Outpouring is distinctly different from Toronto and Pensacola revivals though it includes the characteristics of the previous revivals. Throughout revival history, most episodes of revival had previously been primarily outreaches to lost individuals, and incidentally the church was touched as well. It was generally assumed that the church was not in need and that most of the problems of our lives revolved around the sin in the surrounding world. God is bringing a major shift to the Body of Christ with the message and ministry birthed in the Smithton Outpouring. It became obvious early in the revival that the focus of what God was doing was not first reaching the sinners of the world but bringing revival to the lukewarm church.

Pastor Steve said, "When the revival began, I thought that it would be evangelistic, ministering to prostitutes, drug addicts, hurting people of the streets, but that did not happen. When I started looking at who was coming to the services and what was happening, I realized that God was doing a different thing here. Most everyone coming was just regular church people. People who were desperate, broken, hungry and hurting. They were born-again, but their lives were a mess, and they needed to be rescued. My congregation and I had to come to terms with the fact that we were not having an evangelistic revival for lost souls. It was a revival for born-again people who needed to meet God again, so we took on an "outward focus". We prayed hard, for hours, for God to give us the nations, the cities, our town. We did not launch a media campaign. We simply prayed and the outward focus bore fruit. People want to know if people are being saved. Of course they are. We do not keep numbers because we are focusing on preparing the church for a great awakening. We wanted to create the kind of house that new converts need to live in. We want a house that is not full of hypocrites or conflict or lack of faith."

The emphasis in Smithton is the reformation of the church to the kingdom of God. The Smithton Outpouring is a significant next step in the ongoing revelation of God and reformation of the church. Over the first four years, thousands of pastors were changed, and many have taken the fire of revival back to their own churches. Attendance at the Smithton Outpouring in the first four years was over a quarter million people (250,000) from every state and over fifty nations. They came seeking to be changed in the presence of God. Yet, Steve and Kathy Gray, along with the other servants of God who have been a part of helping birth this move of God, were all just ordinary humble folks who had been touched by the fire of God and became extraordinary in their commitment to the work of revival. The level of commitment and loyalty of these people was extreme, and it was only exceeded by the vigorous life pouring forth from them. Those who stayed didn't seem to miss the natural worldly activities they no longer had time for in the outpouring of the Spirit of God. Everyone moved together as a team in attending the five services each week and serving the many guests who came to be changed. Everyone seemed to some degree to recognize that this was an apostolic work brought forth by God to impact the church and the world with true reformation, and they were more than willing to sacrifice personally to continue to be a part of the outpouring of God.

Some people have had difficulty understanding the intense commitment and loyalty of the Grays and those serving in this move of God. There are different callings and different places of service in the body of Christ. The apostolic type of work necessary to bring forth this awesome move that is touching the world is quite different from pastoring and teaching in a local church. The intensity and level of commitment required is different. One can be a pastor who receives from the movement and then uses the reformed ways of God to serve his local body of believers, or in some other way, one can continue to serve the Lord on a more local basis of meeting the needs of people and seeking to transform one's community to the ways of God. But, if a person decides to be a directly connected part of an apostolic movement like the Smithton Outpouring, the level of commitment will be extreme. Can you imagine the amount of time and effort Paul and the other apostles spent during the transitional time of the first century outpouring of the Spirit of God? Even Jesus and the disciples with Him at times did not have time to eat and have normal rest.

In the Smithton Outpouring, God sent a move of real life purity, holiness, and power upon the earth bringing the seeds of the kingdom of God lifestyle to reform the church and change the world. The coming together of the fire of revival and the Word of the kingdom was, and is yet, being brought with clarity and power to believers and church leaders around the world. The Smithton outpouring was a balance of the miracle working, soul saving, delivering and healing power manifestations of God and a pure revelation and scholarly presentation of the living Word of God. Steve's preaching continues to be well received and seems to be infused directly into the hearts of the people in the presence of God. Steve always has a fresh word from God and almost never repeats a message. The Smithton Outpouring was, in its beginning, the next move of God and is yet planting the seeds of the kingdom of God lifestyle and bringing reformation to the church.

The Smithton Outpouring is not just an intercession church, nor a prophetic church, nor an evangelistic church, nor a miracle and gifts church, nor a Word emphasis church. It is not focused on healing, nor inner healing, nor deliverance, nor prosperity, nor is it focused on social and family issues, but it is clearly focused on honoring God and seeking the kingdom of God first bringing Christ centered revival and reformation to churches. All of the many secondary emphases are dealt with without becoming the focus of the church. It seems that God brought a balance of the previous emphases together in the Smithton Outpouring. There are the powerful manifestations of the Spirit, but they are not the emphasis. There is the powerful Word preached and taught, but that is not the emphasis. There is powerful prayer, salvation, filling of the Spirit, physical healing, miracles, emotional healing, deliverance, strengthening of families, restoration of pastors and leaders, prophesy and other gifts, but none of these things are the emphasis of the powerful balanced move of the in-breaking kingdom of God in the Smithton Outpouring.

At the Smithton Outpouring, the church in general is not preached as right and all the rest of the world free game for bashing from the pulpit. Purity and holiness are practical and real goals, and the preaching does not consist of bashing the lost and sinful people of the world. Rather the church is seen as the focus for revival, and when revived, the church can help bring real change to the hearts and lives of the needy people of the world. The emphasis at the Smithton Outpouring was, and is, the revival and reformation of the worldwide church. God is bringing His church out of the lukewarm, halfhearted state of the past. The message of the Smithton Outpouring is pure devotion to Christ, which brings intense loyalty and total commitment. It is a message of loving God with your whole heart and giving yourself to Him. This message is greatly impacting people in the church who wanted to go to heaven but didn't want a real relationship with God. The world has begun to taste the in-breaking kingdom of God flowing through the Smithton Outpouring. The impact of the kingdom of God lifestyle is destined to affect the world. The church is being reformed and the whole world is being touched as powerful revival continues by the outpouring of God's Spirit through the Smithton Outpouring and a multitude of other ministries and churches touched by the flow of God from a tiny farm town in Missouri USA.

CHAPTER 4

The Pastor's Conferences

The person on the other end of the phone conversation was cheerful and friendly as she gave out information regarding the up coming first ever pastor's conference at the Smithton Outpouring. She was clearly excited about the hundreds of phone calls she was receiving from pastors registering for the conference. For over two years the reports had been coming out of the Smithton Community Church and reaching the eyes and ears of pastors and Christians around the world through magazine articles and news reports. But probably the most powerful communications regarding the outpouring of God in Smithton were the testimonies of those people who had made the trip through the cornfields of the Midwest to visit the outpouring. Even with the reports coming out, most were still surprised by what they encountered at Smithton.

It seemed to most; from the stories they had heard of the tiny Missouri farm town with no gas station and not even a coke machine, that there would be a rural and maybe somewhat corny essence to the revival meetings. And of course, there is the preconceived ideas from other revival meetings, ranging from the typical southern three nights with and out of town evangelist, to the massive renewals that had hit a few years prior to the fire fall in Smithton. For most people nothing they had seen or experienced could have fully prepared them for the encounter with the presence of God and the people of His presence bringing forth the work of God with great focus and spiritual effort. The focus was squarely on God and you. The effort was all about bringing forth His presence and getting that presence to you and in you. No one was showcasing his or her gifts or talents. No one was building anything and no one was trying to get something from you. It was really all about God and getting you together with Him. There was neither country twang nor worldly taint to anything. The Spirit of God moved powerfully through fresh and spiritually powerful music, much of it written by the people of the revival who were playing and singing the praise and worship music. Some who played did not play or sing before the revival hit and were supernaturally gifted to play. The worship leader Eric Nuzum was a fork lift driver before revival and now flowed with the waves and moves of the Spirit leading thousands of seekers and worshipers into a place where the presence of God could consume them.

The one word of description heard most often from those leaving from a weekend at the Smithton Outpouring is, "AWESOME!" When you consider the full meaning of the word it is very appropriate. The meaning of the word "awesome" has to do with both fear and glory. Some synonyms given by Webster's are "inspiring, majestic, magnificent, wondrous, formidable, astonishing, amazing, breathtaking, overwhelming, stupefying; fearsome, fearful, frightening, terrifying, dreadful, alarming, disquieting, perturbing, intimidating." The presence and power of God at Smithton could be all those things, especially to the first time visitor.

One young man who came to the outpouring services for the purpose of mocking was seen running out of the building and down the street at a full run. Later when asked why he left, he replied, "Didn't you see that giant angel walking down the isle toward me?" Not everyone has that kind of an encounter, but coming into the presence of an all-powerful, glorious God can be fearful as well as glorious.

A TOUCH FROM GOD OVERCOMES FEAR

Barbara came to the Smithton Outpouring's first pastor's conference from North Carolina. She had been involved in a major denomination for over thirty years, she served as an associate pastor of her church. She was sure that there was not anything more of God that she did not already have and only came to the pastor's conference because someone else talked her into it. The first day she wanted nothing to do with the things she saw or the people involved. It all seemed strange, unorganized, and unnecessary to her. The prayer time was particularly frightening as people prayed with strength and some of those receiving prayer fell to the floor, flew backwards, shook, jerked, cried, or looked like they were dead. Despite her initial misgivings, Barbara later testified of that the prayer ministry time had changed her life. After encountering the presence of God and receiving a touch from Him during the praise and worship time, she became willing to go for prayer. She said it was like the praise and worship had opened the heavens over her, and she wept and sobbed and told God she was willing to be changed and wanted more of Him. She literally felt a hand on her shoulder, yet there was no one there. She was forever changed as God revealed more of Himself to her and she said later that for the first time she really knew the love of God in a personal way. In her words, "It was like the difference in just dating and getting married. What I had before was like dating Jesus, but now we are one and I now experience His love, not just know about it."

Barbara experienced something that many others have testified of that seems to be one of the benchmarks of this outpouring. While receiving prayer ministry, she physically felt something being removed from within her and then the empty place being filled with the love of God. Here is what she said, "The person praying for me began commanding hurt and disappointment to come out of me. I could literally feel something being pulled out of me. It did not hurt as we think of pain, but there was pressure. I could feel things coming out from deep within. When this was finished, the prayer warrior prayed, 'God fill these empty spaces with your love.' I could feel a warmth being poured into me as God changed me within."

THE POWERFUL PRAYER MINISTRY

Hurt and disappointment are not the only things which are removed from lives through prayer. Many negative and demonic things planted in the lives of people are often pulled out by the hand of God during the aggressive prayer ministry.

The gifted prayer warriors almost never ask the person for whom, they are praying their specific prayer needs. They just begin praying with strength and effort and the Spirit of God reveals the person's need to them. Testimonies are common of people coming to the Outpouring with severe needs and telling no one, yet while being prayed for the needs are specifically addressed. Often when one prayer warrior finishes and moves on, another one will come and begin praying for the same person again, and this may happen three or four times. Later the person will often testify that all of the prayer warriors prayed for exactly the same need though each one had no knowledge of the previous prayer.

After prayer ministry, most of those who may have begun with fear are filled with joy as their lives are changed and they are aware of a significant difference. Often life long weights and limitations are gone. Whether they have been bound by fear, pride, lust, pain, resentment or anger, those bondages that have hindered them are suddenly gone, and the new freedom is obvious to them. In years past, we might have spent months or years in prayer counseling sessions attempting to deal with these things. Now in the presence of God at the Smithton Outpouring, things are met by the power of God and are quickly dealt with. Much of the time everything is not dealt with in one prayer session, but as the people come back and receive prayer ministry several times over the weekend, more and more freedom results.

Chapter 4
The Pastor's Conferences

To the person not experienced in the current outpouring of revival power, the prayer ministry sessions may look very wild, disorganized and strange. Those who have only seen the model of quietly kneeling at the altar with folded hands and bowed head are often shocked by the reality of God and surprised by the very effective results of powerful prayer.

The ministry time usually begins after the Word has been preached. Steve Gray calls for the prayer warriors to come to the front and the praise and worship team to come to the platform. Quietly and inconspicuously, ushers come to the front of each aisle facing the platform and stand shoulder to shoulder blocking the way to the prayer warriors to prevent any overly zealous people from confronting the prayer warriors before the time is right. As Steve completes addressing the gathering, he instructs the people to wait to come for prayer ministry until he says, "Come" and continues to talk to them, further preparing them to receive ministry.

When Steve finally says, "Come now", there is a rush of movement as the ushers move from the aisles and start quickly removing chairs. Some of the people in the front grab their Bibles and pick up their folding chairs and quickly carry them to the sides of the building, clearing all the front half of the room. Others forget about their things and just rush forward to receive prayer. The people stream forward in a mass, and the prayer warriors move out like an attacking army. They are instantly in front of the person desiring to receive prayer ministry. At the same time, a catcher moves quickly from the crowd and is instantly behind the person their assigned prayer warrior is facing, and the prayer begins. Usually no one touches the person receiving ministry, but the warriors are often loud and animated as they powerfully address the needs of the person. Clenched fists, outstretched arms and hands, and violent shaking are common sights as the prayer ministry time moves into full swing. Sometimes the prayer warrior might point a finger toward the body with jabbing motions or move as if they were pulling something out of the person. All the while, their eyes are open wide, fixed and full of strength. They may begin in a somewhat normal voice tone but may quickly shift to shouting loudly, addressing the condition of the person with much power and authority in their voices.

Looking around, you see that a ring of intercessors ranging from four year old children to white haired men have appeared. They stand across the front and down both sides of the building, encircling the prayer ministry area and interceding powerfully for the prayer warriors and the people receiving prayer. The intercessors are assigned the task of calling down the power of God while the prayer warriors are pouring it out to the people. The praise team is now playing and singing full out as a mighty wave of the power of God sweeps through the area, changing lives, cleansing, renewing, healing, and restoring. Soon the prayer area resembles a battleground as people fall to the floor as if mowed down with automatic weapons. Ladies with wine colored cloths move quietly, covering those who are lying on the floor. Some on the floor are perfectly still and ashen in color while some others are red faced and convulsing. Sounds of weeping, moaning, and occasional loud crying blend with the prayer and intercession of dozens of workers in the revival. The prayer warriors and the ladies move about quickly and skillfully from person to person, stepping over the fallen but taking care to not step on them. Some are on the floor for only minutes and others for the rest of the evening. There are no fixed rules as God works, and people respond in many different ways.

As prayer ministry continues, sometimes for hours, a group of youngster from about four to maybe ten years old gather in one corner of the front and begin to roar intercession while some blast shofars, and another wave of power rolls out across the battle field or prayer area.

All of the prayer warriors wear an official prayer tag and have been selected and trained by the ministry. Many of them have prayed for thousands of people, and all of them are spiritually gifted and skilled. They are indeed the foot soldiers, the front line troops that wade in amongst the masses and confront the work of the enemy in them one at a time in literal hand-to-hand battle destroying the work of the enemy. Those who have been changed by the powerful prayer ministry of the Smithton Outpouring have given thousands of testimonies of powerful works of God in their lives.

It does not matter if it is a pastor's conference or a regular weekend outpouring service, the strength and power of the services are the same. However, every meeting is different as the Holy Spirit leads in different ways to minister to the different needs and hunger of the people present.

EXCITING FIRST IMPRESSIONS

People began arriving for the conference several hours before the doors of the Smithton Community Church were scheduled to open for registration of the first pastor's conference. Inside things were being made ready, both in the natural and the spiritual realm. Much powerful prayer had preceded these meetings and continued with strength inside the church. Many of the prayer warriors had, in the past, experienced some difficulties in ministering to some of the pastors who came to the regular meetings. They had found that they sometimes had many preconceived ideas and were not readily open to the flow of the Spirit in a fresh new way in their lives. Others were so accustomed to being the one doing the ministry and giving out that it was difficult for them to just receive. For these reasons, there had been, and continued to be, a very high level of prayer for barriers to be broken through and for the pastors to be very open to the work of the Spirit of God. As the meeting later developed, it became very apparent that their prayer warfare had been highly successful. The pastors were almost all highly responsive and very open to the work of the Spirit. Their hunger for revival and more of God exceeded most everyone's expectations.

One of the first impressions upon driving up to the church was the white gravel parking lot and the parking attendants carefully directing every car to park in a specific place and as close as possible to the cars around it. An unbelievable number of cars were parked in the very inadequate parking lot. The cars were packed in solid with no way for the inner cars to get out until the outer cars left. The attendants all appeared to have a glow upon their faces. They had warm smiles and greetings for everyone. You had the feeling they were looking into your soul and praying quietly for you. You began to feel the love of God in the parking lot.

After parking their cars, people walked a bit briskly to claim their spot in the long line forming in front of the church building. Even the lines were exciting as everyone began to get acquainted with the people around them who were from many states and countries. Soon it was discovered who had previously attended services, and the people around them began asking questions about what they might expect and swapping stories of what they had heard about the Outpouring.

The historic original sanctuary had now been made fresh and new with white vinyl siding on the outside, and everything inside, from the carpet to the nicely padded pews, was bright, fresh, and very clean. When the doors were opened, people began to enter. We walked single file, up the five or six concrete steps through the white door and into the presence of a warm smiling face looking directly and deeply into our eyes. We were greeted with a handshake and sincere questions about who you are and where you are from. The constant eye contact, warmth and sincerity of the person greeting you made you feel at ease. We did not realize that we had already been discerned by the Spirit and briefly prayed for by the greeter. After registration, ushers seated you in the pews in the old sanctuary. A large TV screen was on the small platform behind the registration tables. Attractive plants were arranged about the platform and registration tables. Name badges had been prepared for the pre-registered guest and were laid out in rows alphabetically. Again there was a warm greeting and more eye contact from the ladies doing the registering. Guests were seated in order as they were registered and waited in the old sanctuary while prayer and preparation continued in the converted gymnasium, now made into a revival hall. Conversation continued and expectations grew as the people continued to exchange revival stories and get to know each other a bit.

Then the exciting moment came that one of the ushers stood before the group and began to speak to the eager conference participants. The group quickly quieted and listened to instruction. The usher said we were going to start moving to the main sanctuary and told in what order the rows would leave. By now, the back of the room was filled with standing people, and the lines still stretched down the sidewalk in front of the building. The ushers instructed the people to stay single file and walk as close to the right side of the hall as possible to make room for workers moving about in the hallway. The usher went on to say that they were going to try very hard to get everyone in the main meeting room, but if they could not, the old sanctuary would become the overflow area where the registrants would participate via the large screen TV. The usher also explained that there would be leaders in the room with them.

The old sanctuary was attached to the main meeting room by a hallway that went past the two small rest rooms and several small offices. Just before you reached the end of the hallway, a wide stairway led off to the right down to the basement where the children's ministry was housed. At the end of the hall were double doors leading into what had been a gymnasium and fellowship building before revival. Now it had become the main sanctuary or meeting room for the outpouring services. Not one inch of space was wasted. Folding chairs were set as close together as possible. A small crows nest type balcony above and at the back of the room was used for projectors and sound control equipment. The platform at the front of the room was not a bit too large for all the musical instruments and people who had to be on it. A small nook at the rear of the room was recessed into the back wall with a glass counter in front filled with tapes and other revival resource materials.

As the line moved slowly down the hallway just before entering the open double doors, another greeter welcomed everyone as they passed by, more warm smiles and eye contact. Instantly, as you stepped through the door into the sanctuary, a change in the spiritual atmosphere was obvious to many. They felt the kind of electrifying presence that makes your hair stand up and chills move through your body and your heart knows God is here. Some were moved near tears while others seemed a bit awestruck and yet others seemed to not feel or notice anything. Again you were met and spiritually sized up by a spiritually aware usher who directed you to a seat. Nothing was done randomly, and effort was made to know the Spirit's direction in everything including seating arrangements. After being seated, you realized it was cold in the room as "Big Bertha", the gigantic air conditioner that had been added to handle the packed crowds, poured out cold air in preparation for the heat build up from the mass of closely packed bodies to come. Soon all the seats were filled and chairs added down the side aisles, leaving a very small walkway. Then chairs were added across the back filling up the entire area and leaving a very small walkway to get in and out.

Up front people were standing and actively praying, raising hands and pumping their arms and making other gestures with a few kneeling or lying on their faces. Later even the space where they were praying was filled with chairs. Praise and worship music was playing, and an overhead projector welcomed everyone and gave some information and instructions. Some of the instructions were repeated later as one of the elders came to the platform and welcomed the people. The people were instructed to only receive prayer ministry from the official prayer warriors wearing a prayer badge and to write down words of prophesy and give it to one of the ushers rather than speak it out in the meeting. They were also asked to be sensitive to the neighbors living nearby and to be as quiet as possible when leaving late at night and not slam car doors or talk loudly in the parking lot. They were also instructed at the break to use the bathroom facilities only if absolutely necessary because the sewage system in the small town could not handle the increased water flow if too many people used the facilities. Everything about these meetings was stretched beyond capacity in the small church in the small town. The only thing that was more than adequate was the presence and power of God.

After the room was packed full with someone fit into every space possible, the old sanctuary was still filled with overflow people. The excitement increased as the recorded music continued and some of the musicians began to come to the platform. The people were already standing and worshiping with the recorded music before it was turned off and the live worship team began. It was as if a mighty wind of spiritual power burst forth upon us as the live music began. The people responded with a roar and a shout of praise and were soon jumping up and down with hands raised in sheer excitement of praising a very present God. Soon the floor was bouncing up and down like waves on the sea. One had the passing thought of whether or not the overloaded floor and the reinforcement that had been added could handle the mass of people all jumping in unison. Soon the heat from the mass of highly active bodies had caught up with the air-conditioning system and it was more than warm enough. Yet no one paid much attention to such minor inconveniences for the joy and excitement of praise and worship.

The overflow room did not get left out. The big screen TV and the praise and worship leaders in the front of the room helped bring the anointing into the overflow. The people were just as active and just as loud with their praise and worship as in the main revival hall, plus they had more comfortable padded pews and plenty of air conditioning. The folding chairs in the main hall were the inexpensive, flat-bottom kind that can get very hard after sitting in them for hours. Some folks preferred to be in the overflow, but most wanted to be close to the front in the main revival hall where the action was taking place. The platform and the front of the room were filled with known Smithton people of prayer who not only interceded but also knew how to worship in such a way as to help draw the presence of God.

The many hungry pastors and leaders who had gathered to receive an impartation of what was happening at Smithton in hopes of taking it back to their own churches were very responsive and entered instantly into the lively praise and worship. Those who had come wondering if it was real and if it was God were soon drawn in by the explosion of excitement in worship and praise all around them. The few that did not know for sure why they were there and what was going on looked a bit like a calf looking at a new gate. That is to say, their eyes were big with wonder and had a look of something between amazement and stunned numbness.

LIVES CHANGED FOREVER

The combination of the powerful praise and worship, the testimonies of the people, and the preaching was topped off with the very powerful prayer ministry time at the close of the evening services. The Word brought in the teaching and preaching spoke directly to the reality of the condition and need of the people. The undeniable sincerity of everyone involved in ministering to the pastors and leaders was very impressive and tended to cause even those with hard shells around their hearts to begin to open up. The testimonies of the ordinary men and women of the outpouring soon revealed their true humility and loyal commitment to God and to the revival. They lifted up a standard of innocence and loyalty that could only come from pure devotion to Christ. They modeled a powerful yet humble Christ-like spiritual life that was a challenge to everyone, even before the demonstrations of power flowing through them was evident. For many pastors, it was as if they had entered a dream world, or maybe come into realms of heaven. Hope began to be renewed that had been lost through the years. Hope for things they had desired to see and longed to experience in their own lives and to bring forth in the people of their churches. Doubt and unbelief began to be dealt with as the powerful presence of God captivated their souls. Steve's realistic preaching of the Word and encouraging reports of what God had done in him and his congregation built faith upon the hope that was coming alive.

By the second day, even most of the hard hearts were bursting open and personal repentance led to personal cleansing. Prayer ministry times became more powerful as men and women opened themselves to the Holy Spirit flowing through the prayer ministers. Soon religious spirits were being addressed and eliminated as prophetic prayer and spiritual warfare began pulling down and throwing out strongholds of the past. Deep-rooted things were being removed and the space vacated filled with the love of God and fresh vigorous life. The Word now fell on fresh softened ground and took root quickly. Impartation of the spirit of revival set hearts on fire. Physical manifestations were everywhere, but according to the testimonies later, manifestations seemed to be heaviest on those who had previously said they would never do such things as falling, shaking and crunching.

The pastor's conferences were a great success and have continued to have great impact on many churches. Many pastors and leaders return to Smithton for additional regular weekend Outpouring meetings, and they often bring people from their churches to experience revival and be changed. The revelation of the Word of the kingdom preached by Pastor Steve in the fire of the Smithton Outpouring is spread across the world as many pastors regularly receive tapes of his revival messages and glean from them for their own congregations.

THE FIRST WOMEN'S CONFERENCE

One of the most powerful meetings ever was the first women's conference held in Smithton. The number of reservations coming in soon alerted the Smithton staff that they were going to be overrun. Even with packing all they could into the main revival hall and the old church building used for overflow, they were going to be overfilled. Arrangements were made with the Methodist church about a block or two away to use their building for additional overflow. A TV cable was run temporarily to the Methodist church and large TV monitors installed. Workers were assigned to help with praise and worship and prayer ministry in all the overflow locations.

Chapter 4
The Pastor's Conferences

The Methodist church pastor and congregation were one of the few in the area that had begun to embrace the revival taking place at the Smithton Community Church. Even before the conference, the worship and praise had become so lively at the regular services in the old Methodist church building that signs had to be posted saying "No Jumping". The building was built it the mid 1800s, and the plaster was cracking off the ceiling in the basement and the structure was in danger from the people jumping. This was quite a change from the very quiet services that had been the norm for many years in the old church, but it had not always been so. I noticed a stained glass window given by Grandma Warren. I asked the pastor about it. He said that several years ago when he had come to the church he also was curious about it and asked the people in the congregation, but no one would tell him anything about it. He dug into the old church records and learned that Grandma Warren was a bit of an embarrassment to the church. She had been a girl during the old Cane Ridge Revival days when the church was alive with revival. She had lived long after the revival fires died in the Methodist church, but she continued to run, and shout in church when the Holy Spirit moved her even though the church had long since become very quiet and dignified in its worship style.

The women and the few men who attended this conference will never forget it. When looking back, some still talk about it from time to time. This was not a sweet inner healing thing or a "How to Please Your Husband" seminar, and it did not feature shopping trips for the ladies. This was a serious revival time for spiritual business to be done, a real outpouring of God's power with focus on getting things cleaned out and put back together and moving into real revival. The conference could only be described as explosive. The praise and worship was awesome, but the explosive preaching of Kathy Gray that could turn at any moment into an outpouring of power like a rushing wind was the strength and highlight of the conference. As the power of God swept in upon the women, whole sections of women were suddenly blown down in a single sweep by the Spirit when Kathy prayed and moved her arms toward them from the platform. Some literally flew backwards several yards and crashed into chairs but were not hurt. Arrangements had been made for some of the men to come in and help as catchers during the prayer ministry time. They were summoned and came in the back door only to fall themselves under the power of God. Many of the women could not leave the building when the ministry time ended. They were too overcome with the Spirit of God working in their lives and remained until time for the next meeting. Some who tried to leave were so disoriented and so overcome with the power of God that they had to be led down the steps and were not able to drive. The healings and release of all kinds of limitations were extreme as God did a mighty work in releasing His daughters into revival. Steve's preaching in the evening services was liberating and challenging. The limitations to women moving into revival and becoming what God intended were methodically torn down and destroyed. The women were challenged to move out in faith to their destiny instead of talking about it and making excuses.

The women's conferences continue to be a major highlight of the revival. Some believe, as do I, that Kathy Gray is destined to have a major role in the restoration of women in revival across the world. The outpouring of God is very evident in the vigorous life coming forth through her and is highly contagious to other women. The Word she preaches is fresh and powerful and has made room for her as a major voice in revival, especially to women. Her devotion to Christ and to Steve brings great stability to her spontaneous, explosive personality and ministry. The people of the Outpouring receive impartation and reflect the life and Word flowing through both Steve and Kathy.

CHAPTER 5

The People of The Outpouring

My personal experience at Smithton began at that first pastor's conference approximately two years after the beginning of the Outpouring. One of the most impressive things to me and to most people, especially pastors or others who have worked with people, is the commitment level and loyalty of the people serving at the Smithton Outpouring. Something really wonderful had happened in the season of visitation that had come upon this group, which had grown to number two to three hundred people. When there is no visitation of God, it is hard to get people to church once or twice a week for an hour or maybe two at the most. These people, after two years at Smithton, were in church five times a week often for many hours until the wee hours of the morning. They were vigorous in their worship and service, and they expended unbelievable amounts of both spiritual and physical energy and strength.

These were not paid staff but willing volunteers. They had regular jobs to earn a living and families that needed their care. The whole family actively participated in the Outpouring, and many had become spiritually powerful prayer warriors and served in several capacities in and out of the meetings. They were always at their post faithfully, doing their assigned job at the prescribed time. In addition, they were always at prayer and training sessions. If for some desperate reason someone could not be at his or her post, someone else was designated to fill that spot. There were many jobs to be done to care for the thousands of guest that were coming. These jobs ranged from cleaning the carpet and the bathrooms, to parking cars, greeting the people, and ushering. Other people were responsible for security, sound and video, office and management duties -- including making countless arrangements, answering hundreds of phone calls, and attending to banking and financial matters. During the actual services, some would sing or play an instrument in the praise team, intercede at the meetings, serve as prayer warriors, teach and minister to the infants, toddlers, and the four and five-year-olds, or speak at the daytime conference sessions, and on and on goes the list. If any of the many jobs were not done, the guest would not be properly served and might be distracted from finding the presence of God to change their lives. That would break the hearts of the workers who live for the presence of God and seeing others come into that awesome place of revival life that they walk in daily.

The question most often asked of the people is, "How do you do it?" The answer most often given is, "How could we not do it?" Knowing the reality of the presence of God and experiencing the kingdom of God way of life, how could one not do all in their power to bring everyone possible into such a glorious life? Yes, it is true that laundry may not always be done on time, and the yard may sometimes be a bit late in getting mowed, and the TV almost never gets turned on, but how could they live for anything less? The children are another whole story.

CHILDREN IN THE OUTPOURING

For anyone living in modern American culture which is not too different from any developed nation at this time, it might not seem possible that children could be so on fire for God that they really don't miss the soccer games and hanging out at the mall and experimenting with all the things of the world. Yet that is how it is at the Smithton Outpouring. Children don't have to be entertained if they are trained to flow with the power and life of God.

There is no nursery at the Smithton Outpouring. There is an infant and toddler revival ministry. Training in spiritual matters begins at birth as the infants are arranged in their infant carriers and ministered to by spiritual leaders as praise and worship music is played. The leaders and workers in the children's ministry are very devoted to developing the foundation to support the destiny of God in these infants and toddlers. They recognize that these youngsters growing up in the presence and power of God have a destiny in God that exceeds their own. The children grow up knowing it is natural to be devoted to God and to seek His kingdom first. They feel natural moving in the power gifts of God. They will be more able to carry revival to the churches and to the world than we are.

When the toddlers are able to sit and stand, they are removed from their infant seats and are each given carpet squares on which to stand or sit at praise and worship time. They are encouraged and helped to participate in raising their hands and entering into active worship. They are being prepared for entering the regular outpouring service for praise and worship at the age of four. The four and five year old children remain in the main revival hall for the entire time of sometimes several hours of praise and worship and whatever ministry might take place. Usually before the offering and preaching of the Word, they are dismissed by the pastor and leave with their leaders and helpers. They are then involved with revival ministry at their level for the rest of the service.

The children become powerful and effective prayer warriors and are prepared to begin to participate in the awesome revival services by the time they are six years old. Those who are ten to twelve years old are often powerful in ministry to others. It is not unusual to see the children praying for adults with great power and effectiveness. Some visitors are surprised by the power of prayer emanating from the children and young people. Many times people who are not accustomed to this mighty move of God and have only the reference of irresponsible, lethargic, spoiled and self-willed average children of modern culture cannot understand how the chil-

dren can be so different. Some suppose the children must be un-
happy and regimented to a point near abuse. Nothing could be further from the truth. These children love the presence of God and
love to worship and praise the Lord full out. They are very fulfilled
in the wonderful kingdom of God lifestyle and enjoy the good spiritual food they have eaten since they were babies. They think it
natural to move in spiritual gifts, pray with power, and walk daily
in the Spirit. Most people are not accustomed to seeing godly children growing up in the power and presence of God. They are accustomed to seeing Christian children growing up in a lukewarm
church, raised on a mixture of token spirituality and worldly self-
seeking values, trained in idle entertainment, self-indulgence, independence, and competitiveness. They just do not have a reference in their minds because most have never before seen children
raised in the pure environment of the love of God.

The people at the Smithton Outpouring have made two major
discoveries regarding the children. **They discovered that the children do not have a junior size Holy Spirit. They have the same
Holy Spirit that adults have and can move in the Spirit with
the same power. Secondly, they discovered that children develop an appetite for what they are fed.** In the natural, if children
are fed junk food, they will have only a taste and appetite for junk
food, but if they are fed good wholesome nutritional food with lots
of vegetables, grain products, and other good things, they will have
an appetite for the wholesome foods. This is the same in the spiritual realm. If children grow up from birth with real kingdom of
God life surrounding them, they will have an appetite for the things
of God and not the things of the world. However, if a child has
grown up on worldly lifestyle and only lukewarm church life, he
will have no appetite for the things of God.

The People of The Outpouring

The people of the Smithton Outpouring put energy into worshiping and praising God. They seek with their whole heart to give their all into every service, every song, and every prayer so that every work of ministry is done with great energy. The children are trained to give their energy into worshiping God as well. Families often join the revival after their children are beyond the infant and toddler stage. These children will often already have received some training in lukewarm religious practices and may already have some appetite for worldly ways and things. They must be retrained and helped to develop an appetite for the things of God. This usually does not take long as they are drawn by the Spirit and easily involved in the energetic worship. Parents are taught to teach their children that the kingdom of God is to be put first in their lives. The parents may tell their children who wish to participate in sports and entertainment activities that they must have energy for worshiping God. If they do not have energy to worship God in strength, then they will need to conserve their energy and not expend it in other activities. In other words, if you don't have energy to worship God with strength in church, you don't have energy for sports or entertainment.

MEN OF THE OUTPOURING

The men of the Smithton Outpouring are the strength of the revival and loving heads of the family units. The Outpouring has drastically changed the lives and priorities of these strong men of God. Many of them were once highly career-motivated men with goals of worldly achievements. The single most impressive element of these men is their singleness of mind. One thing is top priority and one thing only — seeking first the kingdom of God and His righteousness. Careers have taken a back seat and are of less significance than revival. Good paying jobs are often left in favor of one that is more compatible with the revival schedule. These men are willing to lay down anything to be a part of the revival that is touching the world and bringing reformation, power, and life in churches. They see raising their children in revival and helping their wives to be all they can be in serving God of more importance than acquiring more things or having an easier lifestyle. Sometimes men must travel hundreds of miles to get back from work situations to be at their post of service at the proper time for the outpouring services. Sacrifice is not a strange word but a daily companion of these men who seek God above all else. To them, however, it is not sacrifice but privilege. The benefits are far greater than the cost. To see their families living for God, worshiping Him with energy, and missing the pitfalls of growing up in an ungodly culture is more than enough reward. Add to that the privilege of being a part of bringing revival of the real ways of God to the world, and of being in His presence, seeing His glory, and being touched and changed by God, and the rewards become so great that the cost seems insignificant.

To see these men give testimony at the pastors' conferences is highly stirring as they reveal their souls and the power of God begins to move. The pastors are stirred as they realize that they themselves need more of what these men have; and they dream of having men like them in their churches.

One of the men is a career Air Force officer. He told of how he had set his goal in life to pilot one of the prestigious B2 Stealth Bombers. Despite all of his efforts to be selected as a pilot to fly one of the very few elite planes, he was passed by for years. He had put his hopes in this one dream. Finally when the time was right, he received the call to come to an air base near Smithton to enter the Stealth Bomber program. Now after being at the Smithton Outpouring for a season and experiencing the power and presence of

God, he realizes that the outpouring of God was the purpose for the move, and flying the B2 is almost insignificant. As this servant of God continued to speak to the pastors, the power of God began to move on him, and suddenly the pastors were all hit with a super-charge of spiritual power. In one motion, hundreds of men shot up from their pews with their hands instantly extended straight toward the ceiling and shouted full out to God. It was as if they all at the same instant had been hit with high voltage, and in one accord, all responded at the same instant. A mighty roar filled the church and flowed out into the community as the power of God moved on us. This man is not a pastor, not an elder, and not tall nor outstanding in appearance, but he is merely a spiritual man working at a job and serving in revival because he has been impacted with the presence of God in the Smithton Outpouring.

Another man earns his living as an auto mechanic. He is by nature a very mild-mannered and quiet hulk of a man, average in height but a bit above average in body build. He shared how he had not been anxious to leave his old ways and enter into revival at first. He spoke with quiet but strong power that again affected the hundreds of pastors. He moves in great strength as a prayer warrior in prophetic type prayer. He looks, to me, somewhat like a predator walking about the prayer floor at ministry time seeking the work of the enemy to destroy. Like fixing cars, he looks for the bad parts and seeks to remove them by the Spirit and replaces them with the love of God.

Another powerful man of God is tall and thin and worked as a civilian at an air base in charge of civilian affairs. He testified that he thought when the outpouring came that he would not be able to participate because of his work. He and the people who worked for him were always terribly behind, and even with his putting in many extra hours, they were not able to catch up the workload. His family had begun to suffer as a result of his working so much and not having time to be with the them. With all of that, there seemed no room for revival meetings at church five or six times a week, but as the outpouring continued and everyone began to be changed, his heart was torn with the desire to be more of a part. Finally it came to the point where he had to decide if he would or would not seek the kingdom of God first in his life. He came to the decision that, no matter what the cost, he would put the kingdom of God first in his life. As he began to participate fully in the revival services, an amazing thing happened at work. Some how God so graced the people that one day one of his workers came to him and said, "I don't know how this has happened, but for the first time ever, I'm caught up with my work and have nothing to do." The workload had not lessened, but the people were able to keep up with the work and were never again far behind. He became a leader and serves as an elder in the church and is one of the very powerful prayer warriors that have prayed one on one with thousands. He and his wife also travel and do preliminary prayer training for churches where Steve and Kathy Gray will minister. He is a power behind the revival as he intercedes and serves as a spark plug in the outporuing services. His devotion and lifestyle are a model for men coming into the Smithton Outpouring.

Another man who is a career military man is a prayer warrior's prayer warrior. He is one of those guys who are sometimes referred to as lightening rods. Some way, if there is any fire around, it will zap the lightening rods first and hardest, and he is subject to being struck at any time. He is average height and medium to slight built and wears glasses. His appearance gives no clue of the spiritual power potential within. He moves in equal spiritual power as an intercessor or as a prayer warrior. He is very responsive to the Spirit and imparts that to others. It is not unusual for him to approach someone to pray and have the person fly backward by the power of God before he touches them. Neither is it unusual to see him very physically active in intercession at pre-service prayer. Having military experience has given him a good base for walking in close responsiveness to the Spirit as well as discipline to flow with authority. Like many people at the Smithton Outpouring, he is an example of ordinary people walking in extraordinary spiritual power in revival.

We have mentioned only a random few of the men of the Smithton Outpouring. There are many spiritually powerful men with similar testimonies. These written here are not the exceptions but more typical of the men flowing in the anointing of revival at the Smithton Outpouring. They reflect the extreme level of commitment, loyalty, humility, and ability to respond to the Spirit and to flow in the power of God. These are men of spiritual strength and sensitivity. It is not unusual to see them respond to the Holy Spirit in powerful manifestations or to see them weeping with compassion for the needs of others or at their own sense of unworthiness in the glorious presence of God. These men are not only committed to revival, but they are also available to father their children with training and encouragement that only a father can give. They are men who are willing to lay down their natural instincts to compete and to rule over others in order to become servants to God and to mankind. As long as men like these come together with love and dedication, this move of God will not be stopped and will touch the world. The world is seeing what God will do when men serve Him with their whole heart.

WOMEN OF THE OUTPOURING

Men are the strength of the Smithton Outpouring, but women are at the heart of the revival. Just like there is not a junior Holy Spirit in children, there is not a female Holy Spirit in women that is different from the Holy Spirit in men. God is God working through whomever He chooses to work through. A woman can do every spiritual work that can be done by a man. In the presence of God there is no distinction of gender. Yet, in the natural there is distinction and differences that make each person suitable for specific works.

If there is to be a leader for the women of revival worldwide, it will be Kathy Gray. Her attractive features and slight build don't cover the dynamic spiritual power within. The piercing but happy eyes give away the secret of the vigorous powerful life on the inside, but it would all be given away with her first movement anyway. Every move is filled with life and the dynamics of the Spirit of God as she may literally bounce, jump, and turn about all with great joy on her face in exuberant worship. Just as quickly, she may passionately weep and drop to her knees in response to what God is doing or saying. Kathy is a woman who is so filled with the power and presence of God and ministers with such dynamic enthusiasm that she is a role model for women in revival in the Smithton Outpouring and across the body of Christ. Spiritual fire seems to suddenly bolt forth from her causing an explosive impact to change lives. Her powerful prophetic prayer ministry seems to reach into the guts of the person and pull out what needs to be removed from the life and replace it with the love and life of God. Her preaching is with immense sincerity and deep emotion, fired with prophetic revelation and scholarly wisdom. She is known to suddenly come off the platform and begin to release spiritual fire to the people sending many flying backward and others crumpling to the ground, sometimes wailing or crying out as God changes them and frees them of life-long bondages or imparts a fresh anointing to them. Kathy has been set free in revival from old personality traits and hindrances, and she receives from the anointing that has come upon her husband. She is able to allow God to flow through her full out, without restraints and resistance. Kathy imparts this anointing and vigorous life to the people of the Smithton Outpouring but especially to the women who often become powerful prayer ministry warriors. Praying with the same powerful anointing, these women minister to the thousands of women guest who come to the Outpouring.

One of the women who has fully received of this anointing and is involved in almost every phase of the ministry is Kathy's assistant. She and her husband have been in the Smithton Outpouring since before the fire fall and are powerful in prayer ministry, having personally prayed for hundreds if not thousands of individuals in the outpouring services. He is a powerful prayer warrior and also is business manager, working closely with Steve on business matters. I once heard Kathy's assistant lovingly referred to as the smiling bulldog because she moves with such graciousness but she will not quit until the desired results are accomplished. Whether it is a spiritual or a natural matter, she will not turn loose until the job is done. She is a very educated and sophisticated young woman and was one of the first to receive powerful spiritual manifestations such as violently shaking in the early days of the Outpouring.

One of the most powerful prayer warriors that I have seen move about the prayer ministry floor is a single mom. She has received greatly from Kathy's anointing and moves in awesome spiritual power in prophetic prayer, destroying strongholds and bringing freedom to many women. She came to the Smithton Community Church over three years prior to the fire fall and says today that she and her family were very messed up and a difficult challenge for the church. She jokingly says that she is the reason revival came to the Smithton Community Church, she and her family were such a problem they had to get a spiritual outpouring to be able to deal with them. Sadly, her husband did not make it through and has been gone for years, leaving her a single mom with three boys. She says that she literally struggled to survive from one service to the next and was kept alive by the spiritual life she received in the outpouring services. She has been completely restored and powerfully changed in revival and imparts what she has received freely to women who come for prayer in the revival. Such power flows from her as she prays that at times she looks almost wild eyed with passion for Jesus and warfare for the people.

Another faithful and powerful prayer warrior is a wife and mother. She and her husband instruct in the prayer ministry and have held many responsible jobs throughout the Outpouring. She always seems to be able to be in touch with God and pull the spiritual power down from heaven to change lives. She is mother to six children, from young teens on down, and yet she is involved in every revival service as well as doing a lot of administrative things around the church office and still finds time to write the Outpouring Times newspaper.

Her young teen twin daughters, began to be powerfully used in prophetic praying at only ten years of age and are yet involved in every outpouring service and youth activity at the Smithton Outpouring. People were amazed to see these young girls with slight builds and long, fine blond hair so powerfully pray and minister that the entire congregation was impacted as though the floor was shaking.

There are dozens if not over a hundred powerful women who carry a large amount of the spiritual ministry at the outpouring. We have mentioned only a few examples. They are humble ordinary women who have received and extraordinary anointing in the phenomenal outpouring of the incredible power of God in the Smithton Outpouring.

LEADERSHIP OF THE OUTPOURING

Steve Gray is the anointed and chosen leader for this move of God, and Kathy Gray is beside him reflecting his anointing and adding vigorous, explosive life to the leadership team. I don't know what I expected Steve Gray to look like after hearing of the spiritual power of the Outpouring, probably the expected image was something of a Saul type, perhaps a tall and kingly looking person or maybe a Superman type. Steve at first glance might more resemble the Clark Kent or the David model. He is a powerful man of God in nice but regular street dress clothes, who is not tall but not really short, and not thick but not really thin. He does not have thin hair, but neither is it glorious, neither gray nor silver, but not really blond either. There is nothing striking in Steve's appearance to give away the underlying power of God. Steve in the natural is neither a social magnet nor a fascinating personality with a lot of natural charisma. There is nothing natural about Steve to account for the great move of God. It is only Jesus, the Spirit of Christ indwelling and flowing through Steve and Kathy Gray that brings forth the dynamic and powerful preaching and ministry. One thing that can be identified in the Grays is a very real and very practical hope of glory. Hope, in the biblical sense of "confident expectation" of God's glory coming forth in the church and in their lives, seems to have been planted in Steve early in life and has provided a place for faith to focus and has produced their destiny. I believe the mystery of the riches of glory of the Smithton Outpouring and the Grays can be solved in one phrase: *"Christ in you the hope of glory."*

Col 1:27: *To them God willed to make known what are the riches of the glory of this mystery among the Gentiles: which is Christ in you, the hope of glory. NKJV*

I Saw The Smithton Outpouring
(Revival On A Small Planet)

As I have watched the ministry of Jesus flow through Pastor Steve Gray, it is very apparent that there is not much of Steve left, and the Spirit of God has freedom to guide and move. Steve is an ordinary man who has found the way to get himself out of the way enough that Jesus can do extraordinary things through him. I once heard a pastor say after being told about the revival in Smithton, "I met Steve Gray once at a convention. If that guy can have a revival, any of us can." I am again reminded of what Pat Robertson said, "Steve, you have taken away all of our excuses for not having revival." A man from Singapore told me while visiting the Smithton Outpouring, "I just can't get over that you people from the small town in Missouri, from one church, can touch Singapore and nations around the world with revival. You, way over here, are affecting us and our churches on the other side of the world."

It is awesome to watch the Spirit of God flow through Steve in guiding the Outpouring services. It seems that each move is perfectly timed and flows as a stream naturally carrying the people to the Spirit's desired destination. When Steve first enters the outpouring service, usually during the praise and worship, there is an instant uplift in intensity though he does not go immediately to the platform and most do not even know he is there. Steve rarely seems relaxed when he enters but usually moves about the front like some sort of spiritual radar data gathering machine, spiritually taking the temperature of the meeting and the people who are there, checking out the sounds coming from the sound system and many details of the whole thing. He may kneel up front or close his eyes for a season as he seeks to hear the Spirit's moving and God's desire for the service. The plan that was made before the service is always subject to on the spot changes. The praise and worship leaders and ministry team are attentive to Steve for directional changes that may come forth at any moment.

Steve believes in preaching to the people who are there and not preaching about those who are not there. It doesn't take long in listening to the sermons he preaches to hear fresh revelation and greatly increased depth to the Word as it is presented in context. You understand how people could tell after hearing the first century disciples that they had been with Jesus. The anointing of the anointed one (Jesus) is obvious.

Steve and Kathy have wisely sought to surround themselves with anointed people to function in the growing leadership responsibilities of the Smithton Outpouring and the World Revival Church. The people involved in top leadership are first of all people whom Steve and Kathy can safely trust. Before their gifts and abilities are considered, the issue of trustworthiness must be considered. The first question is, are they safe people to Steve and Kathy, safe people to God, and safe people to revival? Can they be trusted to honor and maintain the reputation of God, revival, Steve and Kathy, and others in the church leadership? No one becomes involved in the top areas of leadership until they are well known to the Grays and others in leadership. A good reputation at some other ministry will not open the door to leadership in this ministry. There must be personal relationship and connection developed over time to become part of the leadership team. No one is allowed to become part of the leadership until everyone in leadership has some opportunity to interact with him or her and know him or her. If anyone spots something out of order in the prospective leader, their acceptance into leadership must wait until there has been time for the revival to change them and time to prove the change.

For these reasons, most of the early leadership is blood-related family who are truly moving in revival. Most of the leadership also has more than one function. Like seamen on a war ship, they each have work stations and battle stations. Their work stations are off the platform jobs such as different areas of pastoring the people, administrative and office functions, department heads, business management, ministry school instructors, and so on. Their battle stations are what they do in the outpouring services. They may play and/or sing in the praise and worship team, or they may make announcements, or serve on the prayer ministry team, or lead prayer service, or preach, or some other vital ministry job in the services.

Daniel and Shelly Gray are Care Pastors, and Dan plays electric guitar and sings in the praise and worship team. In addition, they travel to churches all over the nation spreading the fire of revival and bringing their unique and powerful ministry. Shelly sings and moves powerfully and skillfully in personal prophetic prayer, and Dan plays the guitar, sings, and preaches strong sermons of reformation.

Pastor Daniel Gray is Pastor Steve Gray's younger brother. He is one of the original thirteen charter members and has been involved in the Smithton Community Church from its beginning in 1984. Shelly became part in 1988 and she and Dan were married in 1989. They ministered as an evangelistic team in biker-type gatherings and prisons before the fire fall. Pastor Dan is a great guitarist and loves to play blues style Christian music. He has written a number of very powerful and sometimes-comical songs that really expose the lukewarmness and hypocrisy of the church. Dan received a miracle healing in the early days of the Outpouring. He suffered with severe arthritis in his hands and right hip. It had grown increasingly worse until it was very difficult for him to play the guitar. He would ice his hands in a pan of ice before playing and would have to stop after two or three songs and put them in ice again before continuing to play. The pain had become so severe that he called a meeting of the associates of the organizations involved with his prison and biker ministry to let them know that he was not sure how much longer he could continue to play the guitar and minister. About ten weeks after the fire fall during one of the out-pouring services, Pastor Steve Gray was led of the Spirit to call for those needing healing from arthritis to come to the front and receive healing. About ten people lined up across the front, including Dan Gray. As the man next to Dan was being prayed for, arthritis was commanded to go, and Dan felt the power of God move through his body and was instantly miraculous healed of arthritis. His gnarled looking hands were fresh and new looking. When they finished praying for the man next to him and came to Dan, he told them, "I'm already healed. God has healed me!"

Shelly Gray, Dan's passionate for Jesus, spirited, exuberant and lovely wife is a natural in ministry. She demonstrates so much love of Jesus for everyone including the unlovely that it is hard for anyone not to receive from God through her. She is Dan's number one fan and can usually be heard at the front of the church during preaching time as she shouts words of affirmation and encouragement from the front row. Shelly is the daughter of a Pentecostal minister and grew up often living on meager fare in humble facilities. In their home, there was an extreme emphasis on loving, serving, and helping others to the degree of sometimes not having much left for the family. She reflects that upbringing with sincere empathy for everyone in need or pain. Her empathy and genuine enthusiasm and Dan's godly wisdom and practical interpretation of spiritual matters, coupled with his intense and sometimes painfully humorous wit, make them a powerful ministry team. Sometimes it is like the Holy Spirit just sneaks up on people through them, and before they know it, they are laughing at themselves and crying about their religious folly and being set free of their sinful bondages or religious traditions all at one time.

Eric Nuzum is God's man, chosen by Him to lead multitudes into awesome praise and deep worship. I have never seen a more anointed praise and worship leader. Eric leads with his heart and follows the Spirit like riding on the wings of a dove. The praise can roar as the Lion of Judah, or frolic as a gentle lamb at play, or soar as an eagle. At times it swoops up and up, higher and higher to the mountaintop, and disappears into the glory as into the sun. At other times, the worship can become as a spotless lamb led to slaughter, touching every emotion by the Spirit and then moving in great strength with the glorious uplifting of resurrection life coming forth. Kathy Gray works beside Eric and amplifies the move of the Spirit with heart-felt expression, and she will alternately lead out on certain occasions. If one of them misses a beat, the other will fill it in. The entire worship team watches Eric for his signals of change as they flow as one.

Pastor Eric's wife Loree is busy mothering their three children, all less than five years of age at this time. Eric's mom is Pastor Steve Gray's sister Nancy Thomason who with her husband Mike pastors a revival church near Chicago. Pastor Eric looks younger than his years, and he is thinner than he needs to be, probably from the strenuous jumping and leaping he does as he leads worship for hours at least three nights a week. He has short brown hair and never overdresses. Pastor Eric Nuzum has great respect for Pastor Steve Gray and is very devoted to him, impeccably following his lead at all times. Eric was a forklift driver and played the guitar some, but he had never led worship or written worship songs before the revival fire fell. After the fire fell, Steve Gray, who had led the praise and worship with Kathy up to that point, turned to Eric and said, "You are going to have to become the worship leader now." Some of the powerful songs Pastor Eric has written and later recorded with Integrity Hosanna were written while driving the forklift. Recently Eric has become a very capable preacher and goes out to minister, spreading the fire of revival in other churches from time to time.

Chapter 5
The People of The Outpouring

J. D. King is National and International Director of the World Revival Network of Ministries and Churches and plays bass guitar on the worship team as well as preaches from time to time. His wife Bobby is Pastor Steve and Kathy's daughter. Bobby helps with the duties in the Network office but has recently been very busy with their miracle baby born a few months ago. They tried fruitlessly for several years to have a child, and after having a number of medical procedures, they mostly gave up and were considering adoption. Bobby was particularly touched by God during prayer at one of the outpouring services and soon became pregnant with Allison. J. D. has great respect for Steve Gray and is himself a revivalist in the truest sense of the word. He has studied and continues to research all of the outpourings and revivals of history and is always on the lookout for books regarding revival history, especially the old out of print ones that give unique insight into the revivals of the past. In addition to his other duties, he teaches revival history in the World Revival School of Ministry as well as other courses.

Pastors Tom and Diana Trout head up the team of pastors to the local church part of the ministry while Steve and Kathy have general oversight over everything including the local church. Tom & Diana are pillars of stability, protectors of the ministry, and the pastors of the flock. They also oversee the Outpouring services when Steve & Kathy are not there. Diana is Steve Gray's sister. They were here in Smithton when the fire fell on March 24, 1996 along with all the other Grays...Dan and Shelly Gray, Nancy and Mike Thomason, Eric and Loree Nuzum, Tom and Diana Trout, and Tim & Jennifer Dieckmann. J.D. and Bobby King came about a year after the revival started. They are all yet fully involved in revival. After the Outpouring had begun, Tom and Diana pastored a church in the greater Kansas City area for a few years. They returned to the Smithton Outpouring after it moved to Kansas City.

Jennifer Dieckmann and her husband Tim are permanent parts of the worship team as well. Jennifer is Tom & Diana Trout's daughter and takes care of a lot of office work for the Outpouring, including all of the conference arrangements and operations. She is a backup singer, and Tim plays the keyboard. Tim could not play any music before the fire fell, and he had never had anything to do with a keyboard. Although he never took lessons, he was miraculously given the ability to play and has been playing for the worship team ever since.

There are currently only two elders involved in the World Revival Church. One elder who had also been an important part of the Smithton Community Church and the Outpouring did not make the move to Kansas City and is no longer involved with the ministry. One elder is the business type elder and is business manager for the entire ministry, and his wife is Kathy Gray's personal assistant. Together, working closely with Steve and Kathy, they take care of most of the business oversight of the whole ministry. They are also powerful prayer warriors in the outpouring services.

The other elder is not as much involved with church business but is heavily involved in spiritual leadership in the outpouring services. He along with his attractive wife call themselves "second row cheerleaders". They have a very important role of spiritual leadership as a spark plug and model of response in the outpouring services. His powerful intercessory prayer and pushing into the spiritual realm have probably had a greater impact on receiving and maintaining the outpouring of God than most people realize. They have also traveled extensively with and for the Grays in ministry around the world. They often go to the churches a few days before the Grays and prepare the way for them. They are especially used in training prayer warriors to serve in the upcoming meetings.

Another couple are permanent members of the praise and worship team. He is Kathy's assistant's brother, and both he and his wife have been part of the Outpouring from the beginning. He plays bass guitar and she plays the keyboard, adding talent and spiritual life to the platform. She has perfectly groomed dark hair, extremely bright dark eyes, perfect complexion and facial features, and an exciting warm smile that speaks of the love of God without saying a word.

Another couple who are important to the Outpouring, like many others have left all to serve God by serving the Grays and the revival. They have traveled with the Grays and assisted them with practical and spiritual matters on trips. His biggest and most recent job is the building of the large new church building in Kansas City. He had full responsibility under Steve Gray for the entire building process. She handles all the money and the bank accounts for the entire ministry.

Another important couple is the head usher and his wife who is the head greeter. They both are lively in worship and powerful in prayer warrior ministry. They have been a part of the Outpouring since before the fire fall.

Another lady who is an important part of the ministry is hidden from view most of the time, producing tapes or preparing the book table and the many duties of the Audio/Video department. She heads up the audio video and revival resources department. She has been a part of the Smithton Community Church from its beginning. She is unmarried and has continued to faithfully serve the Outpouring.

Another unmarried lady who also lives for the revival is a back up singer in the worship team. She has been a part of the Smithton Community Church since its beginning. She also is extremely faithful in serving in the Outpouring.

There are many others not mentioned here, who are now or have been a part of the revival leadership team. Many things about revival are fluid and flexible as the whole movement is solidly anchored in God but moves with the flow of the winds of the Spirit, advanced or limited by men's hearts and their responses to God's moving. There is the stable and permanent core of leadership in the Smithton Outpouring, but many workers and leaders outside the core group come and go as some grow in spiritual realms of devotion and loyalty and are promoted and some for whatever reasons are only connected for a season. Some are sent out to minister in churches, but others may fall away at times of change for lack of mature devotion and loyalty. As God continues to move the revival forward at the Smithton Outpouring and into the World Revival Church and out to the world, there are seasons of great change. There are regrettably some, who for whatever reasons, do not flow on as the next pages of revival history are written and the revival moves on.

A CHANGE OF HANDS

By the fourth year, the Smithton Outpouring had reached a pinnacle of what it could be in the town of Smithton. Everything about the small church and the small town was overloaded and over stressed by the magnitude of the revival and the masses of people coming. The spiritual foundation had been laid, and the superstructure built as high as it could be on the available resources in Smithton. A mighty season of change was in the wind, and it began to stir the nest like an eagle when it is time for the eaglets to leave the nest and move on to their destiny in life. The community of Smithton became even less tolerant of the masses of people and the noisy services in the midst of their small town. They wanted their town back. Change was in the air, and some of the people of the Outpouring wanted their church and pastor back like things used to be. They wanted the access to the pastors that they once had and the personal attention they once had. Some began to put their self-desires above the mighty outpouring and revival God had sent. A critical spirit began to take advantage of the opening given to it, and bitter criticism and strife developed within some of the workers and leaders of the revival.

Some people who had faithfully served in the first years of the Outpouring began to fall away, and they did not make the move into the next great outpouring of anointing for carrying this to the world. As they left, God began immediately to send in new workers and leaders to fill the places of need in the new world-focused work of World Revival Church.

Steve Gray, **speaking of the church at large**, wrote in his book, When The Kingdom Comes, "Today a change of hands is taking place, from those who have dealt selfishly with the things of God to those who are trustworthy. I don't know how God decided the moment at which to divest certain people and institutions of his kingdom resources and invest them in others, but I am sure it has a lot to do with the conditions of their hearts that we cannot see. I know that God's mercy and patience with men and women are great, and that He does nothing rashly. One of the heartbreaks of being a pastor for many years is watching the 'could-have beens' and the 'should have beens'. Theses are people whom God gave an equal opportunity to be a part of the coming kingdom, but who quit the race. I can think of dozens who have passed through the Smithton Community Church."

Thanks be to God for the hundreds of devoted, loyal, and committed servants of God at the Smithton Outpouring who continue to carry the load of work and leadership, those who recognize the destiny before them and are more concerned about fulfilling their part than their personal desires. Kathy Gray said it clearly, "We have a sense of destiny. We know this is it for us. We are not going to squander it."

CHAPTER 6

The Move To The City

The wonderful outpouring of God's Spirit in the small town of Smithton had been an intriguing story of God moving into a small church in a small town and touching the world with a powerful move of God leading toward reformation of the church worldwide. The story had been catchy enough to capture the hearts of Christians and needy people across the country and around the world. In the first four years of revival, attendance exceeded two hundred and fifty thousand people from every state in the nation and over fifty foreign countries as people made their way through the cornfields to the small church in the tiny farm town. Yet the powerful reality of this move of God had not been taken as seriously by the world as it might have been. It had been hard for some to get past the quaintness of the story to the powerful potential of church reformation pouring through the humble, pure-hearted people of Smithton Community Church.

A great transition was about to take place. The fire of God was moving. Pastor Steve became aware that there were people in the congregation who wanted to go back to being more like things once were. These disgruntled people began to complain and speak harshly and bitterly against him and the revival. Their poison attitude began to affect more people in the congregation. God made it clear to Pastor Steve that the outpouring would fade away and die if they did not move with the fire and leave the town of Smithton.

Steve Gray said, "Looking at the old sanctuary, I remembered all of the things that had happened over the years. I remembered the people, where they had sat and what they had experienced. I realized that this was not my room anymore."

The Smithton Outpouring was coming to a close. The end was in sight for things as they had been, but the mighty move of

God was not ending, only increasing and changing to the next level. Outpouring services were shut down in November of 1999. The Smithton Outpouring was moving from the overwhelmed, over-stressed facilities and community in Smithton.

Steve asked God for a guarantee about moving, "I asked the Lord once for a guarantee that if we moved to Kansas City, revival would continue. His only guarantee was that if we didn't obey, the revival in Smithton would end. We were not moving to be successful; we were moving to be obedient."

A church building had been found in Kansas City and lease/purchase arrangements made for it. The plan was to move in November to the much larger facilities in Kansas City, Missouri. The deal for the building fell through, and the Smithton Outpouring was without a new home. Steve Gray, and others searched and found a suitable building that had once been a large discount store. Plans were made and papers drawn to lease the building, but again at the last moment, the deal went bad, leaving the Outpouring without a home. Weeks turned into months with no outpouring services being held. Although there had been no outpouring services, the Smithton Community Church had continued to meet twice a week and was being further refined and prepared for the major spiritual shift about to take place. God began sending in new people to help carry part of the increased load of hosting and stewarding the move of God as it was growing up and moving from the small town to the big city.

Most, but not all, of the faithful people who had served in the past years stewarding this work of God, grew up with the work and made the move to Kansas City when it was finally made. The search for a home continued, and the focus returned to a 62-acre plot of land on Interstate 470 just inside the Kansas City limits. The piece of land had been looked at previously, but it was passed over in favor of other options of existing buildings that seemed to afford much quicker transitions. Pastor Steve Gray felt pressure to do something quickly since many people had already moved to Kansas City and were now having to commute about 90 miles each way back to Smithton for church services. Eventually over 80 families, around 90% of the people of Smithton Community Church, would make the move, many of them selling their homes, leaving their jobs, and finding new jobs and homes in Kansas City. Though it was a battle to make the move, Pastor Steve and the leadership never for a moment doubted that they were doing the right thing. They knew the move was the will of God.

THE LAST OUTPOURING SERVICES IN SMITHTON

It was decided to have one more weekend of outpouring services in the old facilities in Smithton in February 2000. A Smithton Revival Network meeting was planned and pastors and leaders from everywhere were invited to join members and visitors in what would be the last outpouring services in the old Smithton facilities.

Once more before moving, the frail inadequate facilities in Smithton bounced and vibrated with the awesome praise and worship as pastors, leaders, and friends of revival gathered. The powerful presence of God was yet evident at the Smithton Revival Network meeting held February 11th through the 13th, 2000. It was wonderful to be in the familiar, old crowded buildings one more time and witness the continued powerful presence of God increasing and moving us on to the next level. Twenty pastors and leaders made it all the way from Japan for the meetings along with several new pastors and leaders as well as regular Smithton Revival Network members and others.

There had not been, and would not be, any let down or slow down in the Smithton Outpouring. On the contrary, there was a great sense of increase in this powerful work of God as it was growing up to the next level of the powerful presence of God, bringing reformation to churches in our nation and the world.

Pastor Steve Gray brought a very helpful sermon for anyone seeking to bring people into the current revival. The message, called "Milk, Bread, Solid Food", brought both wisdom from first-hand revival experience and enlightening revelation from the Word. It presented insights that can help prevent some of the difficulties of bringing people from the weak ways of the past into the powerful revived lifestyle of the kingdom of God that is coming forth by the outpouring of the Spirit. The Smithton Outpouring continued to be marked by Steve's fresh and powerful preaching and teaching that opens doors of understanding and changes lives along with the mighty presence of God. It is the Word and the Spirit moving equally in power to transform.

Kathy Gray prophetically ushered in the new spiritual essence and began the redefinition of the Outpouring. The focus of the ministry was changing from a small town phenomenon to the transformation of God's people and reformation of churches. The Outpouring was now becoming a part of changing the course of the world. She literally ushered in the life-changing, world-touching work of God. She began Sunday (the last meeting of the SRN weekend) speaking primarily to the Smithton Community Church people. The title of her message was "The Year of Increase, Part 3", but Kathy finished by bringing forth the smashing, overpowering glory of God. It was one of the most powerful meetings I have ever been involved in. I believe it was a major shift in the coming forth of the pure light of God, removing the shadow of death from God's people worldwide.

As Kathy Gray spoke, the Holy Spirit shifted her into speaking prophetically, not just to the church at Smithton, but also I believe she began to speak a shift of light coming to the world. I had never before known Kathy to speak so powerfully prophetic. She never finished the teaching as the power of God flowed in and began removing the shadow of death and dispelling darkness with such force that there was crying out and wailing. Some, like myself, rushed toward the front as people began quickly dragging back chairs and trying to catch those who were falling. Many, also like myself, were greatly shaken and fell screaming to the floor before anyone could pray for them. It was awesome! I was again changed and know I will never be the same. Again, I felt my own life and ministry being changed. For me, nothing continued exactly as it was before that weekend. The LIGHT OF GOD is coming forth in the world as never before, and the SHADOW OF DEATH will be removed from the church around the world. This was only the beginning of the time for which we had waited, but it had begun!

The spiritual reality of the World Revival Church was spoken forth into the world and was beginning to manifest before our eyes. The major shift from the Smithton Outpouring to the World Revival Church had begun in the spiritual realm. The vision was changing and being progressively clarified. Again, as in the beginning of this move of God, no one truly knew the magnitude of what the future held for World Revival Church.

COVER THE CITY IN GLORY

While praying about Kansas City and what to do about a building, Steve Gray heard from God that He wanted to cover the city in glory. After hearing the Lord's direction to "COVER THE CITY IN GLORY", Steve Gray was pondering how this could be done, and then the obvious plan of God came into view. It was a new thing that helped to demolish walls, destroy competition and rivalry, and spread the glory of God over the city. Steve began immediately to call pastors in the Kansas City area and make arrangements to meet in their church buildings for two weeks on Friday and Saturday evenings and to participate in their regular Sunday service to whatever degree the pastor desired.

The powerful Smithton revival team and the entire congregation, along with guests coming in from around the world, met at different churches in Kansas City on Friday and Saturday evenings, from March 24 until June 29, 2000. Outpouring services were held for two consecutive weekends at each of the participating churches in the southern, northern, western, and eastern parts of the greater Kansas City area.

At the first Cover The City In Glory meeting, Kathy Gray reflected back on what God had done in Smithton, "Look what He did for us, out in the middle of nowhere. Over the past four years now, we have been visited by over sixty nations. Thousands and thousands of people have found their way to a church in the middle of nowhere. We have seen the glory of God. We have seen them lined up around the building, waiting to get inside. I have seen cars lined up for two and a half miles down Highway 50, waiting to turn on Route W. to come to a little old church built in 1859. I have seen times when the people were worshipping God so intensely and my husband would walk among them and they would collapse like wheat blown by a hard wind. He wouldn't touch anybody, and I would just see them collapsing under the glory of God. I have seen the hand of God work so many miracles and healing. Holes in baby's hearts have been sealed up. People who were going to have surgery on their knees were able to cancel the surgery. There was a woman with a brain aneurysm who was becoming a vegetable. She said, 'I am going to go to Smithton'. Here friends almost had to carry her in. She said, 'I am going expecting a miracle'. Nobody knew that.

The Holy Spirit spoke to my husband during praise and worship. 'Someone is here expecting a miracle. Ask for that person to step out into the aisle right now! One of us put our hands on her head. We said, 'Live, live, live, right now!' And she collapsed to the floor. Forty minutes later, that woman was up on the platform standing, speaking glorifying God. We got a report from her doctor the next week, that the thing was gone! I have seen the glory of God. He wants to work. He wants to renew His deeds in our day more than we want it."

The last several weeks of Cover The City In Glory meetings were at a church in Lees Summit where the pastor graciously opened the doors of his church without reservation for the outpouring services. During the time at the church in Lee's Summit, a very interesting story was uncovered. The pastor revealed that on Sunday morning March 24, 1996, an outpouring of spiritual fire fell in their church. This was the same day the fire fell in Smithton about 85 miles down the road in the evening service. He said it was awesome, but they did not know what to do with it and did not embrace it. Now the powerful Outpouring was meeting at his church and had purchased 62 acres of land only a short distance down the road in the same general area of Kansas City.

THE FIRST WRN MEETING IN KANSAS CITY

It was decided to have a Smithton Revival Network meeting and a large outpouring service at a Hotel in Kansas City. On April 11 - 13, 2000, over a thousand people gathered for the "Expanding The Vision Conference," the first major Smithton Outpouring conference in Kansas City. Only now it was becoming "World Revival Network of Ministries and Churches" (WRN) instead of the Smithton Revival Network (SRN). The network National and International Director J. D. King said, "The name change is to more accurately reflect the worldwide aspect of the network ministries. Many pastors and ministers from many countries are in need of the network connection and assistance in spreading revival in their nations."

Dr. Rodney Howard-Brown, internationally known revivalist who is originally from South Africa and now from The River in Tampa Florida, and Mike Bickle of International House of Prayer (IHOP) in Kansas City were the guest speakers. They worked along with Steve Gray and the rest of the Smithton team to minister to the excited gathering of pastors and leaders from across the country and other nations. Rodney Howard-Brown spoke on the anointing, and the power of God was evident as many made commitment to God and many received ministry and prayer. There were powerful manifestations of the Spirit that strongly impacted people and brought healing and restoration to lives and ministries.

Mike Bickle spoke on restoring the tabernacle of David, emphasizing the "harp and bowl" ministry of worship and prayer. The unprecedented sovereign prayer movement now occurring around the world continues to increase as people are being drawn to connect intimately with God in prayer and worship. The International House of Prayer (IHOP) in Kansas City under Mike's direction is now bringing forth continuous live prayer and worship twenty-four hours every day, seven days every week. Interest is high and increasing among other pastors and churches in different parts of the world to begin a continuous 24/7 prayer and worship ministry unto the Lord.

Pastor Steve Gray spoke regarding the presence of God and the need to get rid of "foreign gods" and to incline our hearts toward God. To be carriers of the presence of God, it is important to put away everything "foreign to God" from our hearts and lives. Some things may be familiar to us, but they may be foreign to God — foreign to His righteous ways of doing and being. Joshua in his final message to Israel said, *"Now therefore, put away the foreign gods which are among you, and incline your heart to the LORD God of Israel." (Joshua 24:23)* Just as God would not bring His presence among the people in the day of Moses because they were a "stiff-necked" people and had made themselves another God, He will not bring His glorious presence among "stiff-necked" worldly people today. God would not come among the children of Israel because His holy presence would have destroyed them, but instead He would meet with Moses in the tent of meeting outside the camp.

The regular weekly outpouring services continued to be held at a church in Lee's Summit while a large used tent was purchased, city permits were acquired, and the newly purchased land was prepared to set up the tent. Increased vision for the newly renamed World Revival Church began to come forth, including plans for World Revival School of Ministry and building a large new building to house the church and all of its expanding ministries. A fresh focus of reaching Kansas City and spreading the fires of revival to the world began to grow into place. The Smithton Outpouring was redefining itself as God was bringing a new day. The old was not forever passing away but was giving life as a planted seed to the new plant so it can bring forth the new crop of a greater harvest. God began to send in new gifted and anointed people to carry forth the new worldwide ministry focus, people who were ready to be loyal and committed, and who were humble and teachable.

In this manner, life began anew in the big blue and orange striped tent that stood upon the 62-acres of land on I-470 in Kansas City.

CHAPTER 7

In The Big Tent

The powerful presence of God filled the tent with what I saw as a golden glow. The big tent filled with worshipers and seekers at the first night of services of the Smithton Outpouring in Kansas City. The tent was filled with those who braved their way through the rain softened new gravel parking lot into the old tent with the green indoor/outdoor carpet laid smoothly on the ground. People had come from many states and as far away as Egypt to be touched by God in the Smithton Outpouring that continued with increase at the new location in Kansas City, Missouri.

A sense of history was evident as one reflected on the powerful move of God which began over four years ago. There was a sense of a link with all the great revivals of the past as God continued to meet with His people to renew, revive, and reform His church. Yet even stronger than the sense of history was the sense of destiny. It was in the air. One could not help but feel the spiritual charge of destiny as fresh new history was being made before our very eyes.

The World Revival Church began on the night of Friday, June 30, 2000, in the "tent of meeting" erected on the beautiful 62 acres of land off I-470 in Kansas City, Missouri. The sounds and sights of construction were all around as bulldozers prepared the land where the new building would be built. An old house already on the property now served as the infant/toddler and children's ministry center, and portable rest rooms and mobile offices met the immediate needs of a church on the move. Even during the first meeting, workers were hammering and placing pieces necessary for the night's meeting. The physical surroundings may have given a sense of transience, but the selfless, tireless, joyful efforts of the people clearly declared the permanence of a ministry that was here for the long haul.

I Saw The Smithton Outpouring
(Revival On A Small Planet)

Dedicated workers had worked day and night, and in two weeks, they had seen the miracle of God's preparation of facilities. The electrical company had to design and build a power transmission system sufficient to run the future new building as well as the existing tent. Poles had to be set from some distance away, wires strung up, and transformers installed all within two weeks time. The land had to be graded, and gravel was hauled in and smoothed. The large tent had to be purchased, transported to the property, and placed upon a smooth, hard spot on the land. Then the tent had to be raised on the site and repaired as several holes were found as it was put up. The green turf type carpet had to be laid over the entire floor. A platform had to be built and all of the electrical and sound system installed and connected. Lights were strung up, and four giant air conditioners were purchased and installed. Workers were pushing beyond their normal limits to be ready in time for the first outpouring service on Friday night.

On Thursday evening of June 29, 2000, when the first Thursday night prayer service was held on the land, there was so much work going on inside the tent that the prayer meeting was held behind the tent in the evening shade of the tall trees next to the tent. The leader stood on a chair as the people gathered in close and cried out to God to bring forth His power and presence this first weekend on the land. All the hard work and prayer was for one primary purpose, to provide a place and an atmosphere where God would be comfortable coming down and meeting with His people.

People around the world are looking for a new attitude, an attitude of love and sacrificial service bringing forth the glory of God. As Pastor Steve Gray said, "There is plenty of new wine available in the world today, but what is needed is new wine skins to hold the new wine". People are looking for the real thing. They are looking to give their lives to serve Christ by serving His people. The old half-hearted religious thing is just not an option once the presence and glory of God has been tasted.

History was made on the night of the first outpouring service, and the children and grandchildren of those involved on that historic night will likely speak often of those who gave their lives to become part of the destiny of the Smithton Outpouring / World Revival Church. From the 62 acres in Kansas City in the heart of the USA, the world is destined to be touched as the power of God from Smithton not only remained but also continued to increase. People were continuing to be drawn of God to move to the area and be a part of the move of destiny. God is doing a new thing. It is not the same old "world outreach" label on a self-focused, self-promoting ministry like we have seen in the past. This is truly real people, real nobodies, who are giving all to become a part of the destiny of changing the church and the world.

INCREASE IN THE BIG TENT

There was a notable increase of miraculous healing during those early meetings on the land. One young mother had severe knee problems and could hardly get up and down the stairs to care for her new baby. She suffered continuous pain and loud popping sounds from her knee. She was instantly and completely healed and could not stop jumping about and laughing and crying with joy. Another woman testified of great warmth entering her chest when she received prayer, and her serious allergy problems were gone. No attempt was made to determine the numbers and types of healings. Also no attempt was made to keep up with the number of those born again or the multitudes receiving new life and new power for ministry. Many people, including pastors, gave their lives totally into the hand of God.

Pastor Steve Gray preached from Acts 10 about how Peter was not ready to be sent to Cornelius and had to have an encounter with God to adjust him to make him ready. Many who cry out to be used of God are not yet truly ready and must have an encounter with God to change them and their thinking before being sent to the ministry God has for them. A new wineskin is required to hold the awesome power God wishes to impart to reform the church and reach the world in this day. After the encounter with God changed Peter, he could then say when the call of God came, "Yes, I am he whom you seek". (Acts 10:21)

I felt more able to answer the call from God with that same reply than ever before, "Yes, I am he whom you seek". I am certain that with many, as it was with me, there was new life, fresh anointing, and potential planted within them. Everyone who feels the need for more to do the work and ministry of God needs to receive impartation of the presence and glory of God as it was coming forth from these exciting meetings.

Ministry time was powerful as wave after wave of glory empowered the prayer team with great life and authority over all powers of darkness and every need of the people. We saw the beginning of an explosion of the ministry of God from this place out to the world. We saw increased lives and people being prepared to do their part in bringing change to the church and reaching the world. We got in on some "blue chip" spiritual stock from heaven on earth.

The entire first weekend of World Revival Church services in the big tent in Kansas City were marked by the continuation of the powerful presence of God visiting the services as over the past four years. Only there was increase now that the big tent is up on the homeland. There was an increase in serious excitement of the hundreds of worshipers and seekers. The seriousness stems from the sense of destiny that is prevalent in the spirits of the people and seemingly fills the air.

"Thank God I am alive and get to be a part of what God is doing in this movement." This feeling, echoed by many, was expressed by a restored pastor in his testimony Saturday evening. He is a former denominational pastor who has preached to thousands and now happily sweeps and vacuums the tent floor and fulfills whatever duty needs doing. He shared how he and his wife had come to Smithton seven months earlier, overwhelmed with despair and facing the end of their marriage. He said, "This was my last hope. I knew I would end my life if God did not do something real in Smithton." As a successful pastor of a successful church, he knew all the words of faith and sought to practice what he preached, but something was missing, something was lacking to bring real and vigorous life. God powerfully met him and his wife at Smithton in revival, and their lives will never be the same again. As soon as they drove on the parking lot, the parking attendant powerfully ministered to them with a spiritual word of encouragement, and hope began to be reborn. Soon the power of God began to change them, bringing deep healing and finally vigorous spiritual life. Their new life is evident to all who know them. They are full of joy, deeply in love with each other, and overflowing with the ministry of Jesus by the Holy Spirit to everyone, especially those of their past denominational affiliation. They will surely be used of God to spread the fires of revival in time to come. Many others could have given similar testimonies. At one point during the weekend of services, Pastor Steve Gray asked that all who were now members of the Smithton Outpouring / World Revival Church and had been in full time ministry before they came to stand, and over twenty people stood to their feet.

THE FIRST SUNDAY SERVICE ON THE LAND

The first Sunday service on the "promised land" was full of celebration, promise, and fulfillment. Celebration for what God had done, promise of what He is going to do, and fulfillment in what

God was doing that day, Sunday, July 2, 2000. Recently appointed Pastor Tom Trout led a true revival communion service. This was my first communion at the Smithton Outpouring, and I had wondered what communion would be like in revival. Like everything else in revival, I found it to be the real thing instead of the form we may have practiced in religious services of the past. Eric Nuzum and the praise and worship group began softly singing "Redeemer, Savior, Friend" as the elements were passed out. The music and song built to a crescendo as the elements were partaken of, and Jesus was truly partaken of by hundreds who were more committed to Him than ever and joined in the worship of the song.

Pastor Steve Gray preached from (1 Corinthians 12:1) and following verses. *"Now concerning spiritual gifts, brethren, I do not want you to be ignorant."* Steve pointed out that the word "gifts" is in italics in the KJV and therefore is not in the original text but is supplied by the translators. Much more is being talked about in this passage than the "nine spiritual gifts". God does not want us ignorant of spirituals (spiritual things involving all matter of work and ministry). The manifestation of the Spirit brings gifts and abilities in all areas of service, including the many tasks we consider to be natural things. We are to all work together in the "power of all", each doing our part, in the supernatural power of the manifestation of the Spirit. (1 Corinthians 12:7) *"But the manifestation of the Spirit is given to each one for the profit of all."* The important thing is to hear God and not listen to dumb idols that have no voice but yet can speak to us. Without audible words, the shiny new car can say, "Buy me; you must have me", or those fine new clothes can say to us, "You need me. Look how much more respect you will have and how much more highly people will think of you if you have me", and so on. Along with many other things, money can be a dumb idol without voice that talks to us. We must hear the voice of God and not be led by dumb idols. *(1 Cor 12:2) "You know that when you were pagans, you were once carried away to these dumb idols, however you were led."*

The big tent was filled with excited and sometimes noisy activity from front to back after the service as groups met in different portions of the tent for special purposes. A group of more than fifty new members were meeting in the back of the tent with the pastoral staff, and they strained to hear Steve & Kathy Gray, Tom & Diana Trout, Dan & Shelly Gray, and Eric & Loree Nuzum above the loud prayer at the front of the tent. A group of fiery men and women were praying there as they prepared to leave immediately for the Rodney Howard-Browne Crusade in Shreveport, Louisiana, where they would be a part of the street evangelism and crusade ministry. Also at the front and on the other side of the tent was a group of people receiving special prayer who are in process of selling their houses and moving to Kansas City. At the same time in the back of the tent, visitors and others purchased tapes, books, and CDs to extend the ministry of the outpouring in their home area. While directly in front of the book & tape tables, a line formed of new members to have their pictures made. Steve and Kathy Gray personally greeted them as they moved in family groups to stand before the faded white tent wall to be photographed. Other people waited for directions to a church near Grandby, Missouri where Daniel and Shelly Gray would be ministering on Monday and Tuesday nights. Add to this all the people standing about just fellowshipping with one another and taking care of ministry business, and you begin to get a sense of the living work of God bringing exciting life in the big tent in Kansas City.

OFFERING INTERUPTED

The six months or so spent meeting in the tent were very exciting, and many significant moves of God occurred as increase continued. On one occasion, Pastor Tom Trout was talking to the group in preparation of receiving an offering. Before he could finish talking about the offering, a very welcome interruption stopped him. A woman in the congregation got up and began walking up the aisle shouting, "I can walk! I can walk!" over and over again. She shrieked, "I can walk!" and began walking quickly up and down the aisle and in front of the platform, interrupting Pastor Tom Trout's comments. "I can walk! I can walk!" she yelled as Pastor Eric Nuzum grabbed her hand and ran back and forth with her. "I can walk!" Surprised at the noisy interruption, Kathy Gray hurried off the platform to assist as Eric escorted the excited woman yelling, "I can walk!" When the woman stood next to Kathy on the platform, Kathy asked, "You can walk now?" The lady yelled into the microphone, "I can walk!"

She then related that yesterday she couldn't walk at all on her left leg. She couldn't walk without help and could not go up or down stairs. "Do you know that you just walked up some stairs to get up here?" Kathy asked. The woman looked down the set of stairs for the first time and chuckled, "Oh, I did!" And again excitedly shouted, "I can walk! I can walk!"

Praise and thanksgiving erupted from the 500 witnesses to this miracle. The woman, had traveled from Albuquerque, New Mexico, desperate for a touch from God. She said that she had a severe case of arthritis and gout, and doctors told her that her left leg had to be amputated. She related that when she stepped onto the property the day before the meeting, she felt life tingle into the leg that doctors had pronounced dead.

She testified that she had come to the service that evening and asked the Holy Spirit to knock her out. When Kathy prayed for healing for her, she shook and fell to the floor. As she lay on the floor under the power of the Holy Spirit, God was bringing life to her leg.

Other ladies testified of God's healing power that evening. The Lord swept through these ladies taking away severe pain, opening ears and lungs. One lady had severe chronic pain from fibromyalgia for 25 years. That night she had no pain for the first time. Another lady had severe pain in her lower abdomen that kept her from breathing properly. She was instantly healed and could breathe normally for the first time.

Another victim of severe pain from chronic allergies and a sinus infection testified that her sinuses popped open and she could breathe. Cheryl came to the meeting with excruciating pain in her ear and throat. She testified that the Lord healed her as she fell to the floor under the power of God.

Miraculous healings increased after relocating to Kansas City, in response to the intense prophetic intercession of young and old, and the exhortation from Pastor Steve Gray to lavish worship upon the Majesty of God. In the beginning of this meeting, Pastor Steve had exhorted the people to send messages upward to heaven to pull heaven down here. "The more we make it like heaven down here, the more He responds," he exhorted. "The more we establish His glory, the more we see His power."

As the people abandoned themselves to adoring and loving Jesus, His glory flowed into the tent. Then Pastor Steve stepped forward and called for the intercessors, especially children and youth. As their young voices cried out to God, the majestic power of God fell as people rushed forward to get prayer. Soon the front was strewn with old and young alike lying under the surgical hand of God bringing healing to the body and to the spirit. Indeed, we watched heaven come down and His authority and power being established under the tent full of people hungry for Him.

PRAYER AND THUNDER

Meeting in a tent is exciting; you are much closer to nature, and weather becomes a greater factor. Go with me in your imagination to one of the services:

It's Friday night, and prayers are booming from the pre-service prayer while outside the big tent thunder is booming and rain is pouring down. As some people gingerly walk toward the door, trying to manage their umbrella and avoid stepping into ankle deep streams of water from the pouring rain, others run briskly with only a jacket or something over their heads. Upon entering the tent the presence of God and the excitement of the people makes it all worthwhile.

I remembered seeing the small patches of light through the top of the old tent earlier and wondered if it will hold out the downpour of rain. For the most part, the tent holds and only occasionally is the green indoor/outdoor carpet wet, as a few people later discovered at prayer ministry time when some fell in soft wet spots. Pieces of plastic became a safeguard for some of the electronic equipment, and a man moved out in front of the platform occasionally to lift a portion of the tent with a long pipe and cause the buildup of water to dump before leaking in.

The big tent filled to capacity with slightly damp people from fourteen states and Canada. As the praise and worship built, the rain slowed and again the heavy presence of God filled the place and overwhelmed our hearts with His love and joy. As I listened to the testimonies of changed lives, healed hearts, healed marriages, and healed bodies, it became hard to see my note pad for the tears of gratitude in my eyes. We are so blessed to be a part of the awesome work of God coming forth at the Smithton Outpouring in Kansas City. I am so thankful to have lived long enough and been brought to this place in this glorious time.

Among the many testimonies, I was especially blessed by the story of a group of Methodist pastors. One couple gave testimony for the group, sharing how they had found new life and desired to take revival back to their home churches in their home states. One pastor said, "We have a hunger for God. John Wesley had it, and we want it! And Jesus has said, it is time!"

Decisions were made to serve God as the power of God touched hearts early in the service. Pastor Steve Gray took the microphone and began to speak of our walk with Jesus. He said we have another chance tonight to give our lives to Him. "We have often asked Jesus for things — for blessings. Now we are saying to Him, 'Jesus, ask us what You want, and we will do it.' You must be ready to change anything. He is the king and not you. He just wants you to love Him. The only thing He cannot have on His own without you is you. You may have been lit, but have you been launched? We don't want to go any further in this service until every boy and girl, every man and woman has an opportunity to give your lives to God". The drawing of the Spirit was powerful as hundreds prayed in unison to give their all to Jesus and ask Him to be their savior and Lord.

STORMS THREATEN THE BIG TENT

In several near misses through the summer months, the tent was threatened from powerful thunderstorms when meetings were not in progress. On one occasion, the tent was full when one of those Kansas/Missouri style storms rolled in. God used it to vividly illustrate Pastor Steve's sermon.

I Saw The Smithton Outpouring
(Revival On A Small Planet)

Earlier in the week, Pastor Steve and Kathy Gray had received word that their first grandchild was about to be born. As they were making preparation to leave for the hospital, disturbing news came to them regarding a troubling situation that was not as previously stated and threatened the work on the new building. Steve heard a very reassuring word from God, "Why are you so afraid?" He recognized this as Scripture and prepared a sermon from Matthew 8:23-26, the passage that deals with the storms at sea and the fearful disciples awakening Jesus. To the disciples, it seemed obvious why they were afraid. They had seen many storms before and knew what could happen to boats and the men in them. The tempest was blowing, lightening flashing, thunder rolling, and waves smashing the boat and tossing it around. According to all of their past experiences, it was time to be fearful. What they had not taken fully into account is that Jesus was in the boat with them.

Thursday before this message was to be preached on Friday, as Pastor Steve cradled little Allyson Grace, his first grand child, safely in his arms, he received a phone call that all the troubling situation with the building permits had been completely cleared up with the stroke of a pen.

Friday night, as Pastor Steve was sharing this story and preaching this message, a storm approached, and soon the big tent was flopping in the violent wind as the lightening flashed and thunder rolled and torrents of rain smashed against the tent. The sounds and sights were ominous, everything swaying and popping and creaking and water beginning to splash into the tent in spots. It was very much like being at sea in a violent storm. At one point, the lights went out, and darkness filled the tent while lightening flashed outside its thin walls. In a matter of seconds, the ushers had flashlights lifted up so everyone could see, and in only minutes, the emergency power was on. Men hurried about to cover the equipment with plastic to keep it from getting wet. The service ended prematurely and the people were told that they should go home. Yet some of the people were in no hurry to leave, and some visited while others received prayer ministry.

What a sermon illustration! If these things had happened in a worldly meeting, there would probably have been panic, and people may have been trampled as they tried to get to safety. Yes, there were a lot of people who did get into fear and were faced squarely with the message of the sermon "Why are you so afraid?" Pastor Steve finished the sermon the next evening, and they all ran forward for ministry and were set free.

Pastor Steve made it very clear that our past experiences with storms is no longer valid in this day of visitation, if our life is in the boat with Jesus. If our lives are for His purposes as we walk with Him in this day of visitation, then the old fearful experiences from the past are invalid reference points. We must understand Who is in the boat with us, and we must come to a new understanding of who we are in this day of visitation. The things that wouldn't work in the past can work now, and we do not need to fear things that were once fearful to us. Our old limiting thoughts and beliefs are no longer valid. It is a new day when Jesus is visiting His people as He is in these days.

THE PASTOR'S CONFERENCE IN THE TENT

THE ROAR OF PRAISE

It's Friday night of the Smithton Outpouring / World Revival Church Pastors and Leaders Conference. The big tent at the new home of the World Revival Church just off I-470 in Kansas City is packed from front to back as between 750 and 800 leaders and seekers send up a roar of praise to God. The 110-degree heat of the day outside was no hindrance to the fire of God inside the air-conditioned tent. The corporate anointing was awesome as the crowd roared out song after song and shout after shout, calling for the fire of God. I don't know if others saw the golden glow or if it was just me. It began at the platform and then filled the entire tent all the way to the people standing in chairs in the back.

God marvelously responded to the desperation of the people — people who have gone beyond hunger for God to desperate abandonment of all else for Jesus — just to know more of Him — more of His innocence and purity in our own lives. In many years of seeking to serve Him, I have never known a time like this, a time when so many are so in love with Jesus and when He is so near and so powerful to those who seek Him.

There were massive demonstrations of His love and power. Many were instantly healed of diseases and disorders as waves of healing flowed. A healing team of ministers joined hands across the front and prayed for the groups of people who were gathered before them seeking healing. As the team prayed, the group took one step toward the mass of people, and most of the ones awaiting prayer fell to the floor, many violently. After one group received ministry, another group was gathered until all who were seeking healing had gotten prayer. Kathy Gray took the microphone and prayed against tormenting diseases as the roar of prayer continued.

While many were yet on the floor under the power of the Holy Spirit, some came to the microphone to tell of what God had done. They testified of a skin rash instantly healed — leg, arm/shoulder, and back conditions healed — movement returned and pain gone. One lady, said that after having open-heart surgery she had developed emphysema and had difficulty breathing. When prayed for, she felt a pop in her lungs and could now breathe normally. One man who was still very much under the influence of the Spirit had difficulty speaking and standing, but he managed to tell of having had serious problems with three discs in his back. He said that God had healed him. He heard two pops in his back and a moment later two more, and his back was healed. He said God had done a snap, crackle, pop healing, and he felt really good.

THE MIRACLE OFFERING

Pastor Steve Gray talked of the need for equipment for the ministry to be able to spread the revival on television and asked God for a miracle offering. A pastor from San Antonio, a friend of the ministry, asked if he could speak about the offering. He spoke of the lion roaring in victory and the people roared with truly a miracle offering that completely met the need for TV and Internet equipment. During the miracle offering, a lady who had been in the back resting in the Spirit since the earlier waves of healing, came jumping, shaking, and giving glory to God as she testified of being healed of cancer. About now I am thinking — Wow! What more can God do tonight! But there was yet much more to come.

YOU GIVE THEM SOMETHING TO EAT

Pastor Steve Gray spoke revelation and wisdom into our hearts regarding revival from Luke 9:10-17. God had no problem feeding thousands in the wilderness. He had fed all Israel with manna from the sky for forty years, but the time has changed. The Bread of Life has come, and no longer is manna going to fall from the sky. Now the Bread of Life, Jesus, chooses to use what little we have and **whom He has** to feed the thousands. He took the loaves and fishes and broke and blessed them, but the miracle did not happen in His hands. Not until the bread and fishes were in the hands of the twelve "waiters" (disciples) did the miracle occur. The miracle happened in their hands.

The miracle was from Jesus, but He said to the disciples, "You give them something to eat". He chose to use the small number of "servers" and the small amount of food they had by empowering them to feed the thousands. Revival is a sovereign move of God, but He wants it in your hands. The miracle of revival is in our hands. It is not the time to be looking to heaven for manna to fall. The Bread of heaven has already come down. Don't wait for revival to fall out of the sky. The sovereign move of God is here. The question now is, will we receive it? Will we make a place for Him on earth like it is in heaven?

Moses was told to make the tabernacle like the pattern from heaven. God wants a heavenly copy on earth. We must make a place comfortable for Him. There must be no attitudes in church that are not in heaven. There is continuous praise and worship in heaven. We spend much time in sending up our praise and worship, and then when He comes down, He comes quickly. When Moses got the pattern right, the glory came down and filled the tent.

POWERFUL PRAYER MINISTRY

The ministry sessions were awesome as hundreds received powerful, life-changing ministry from the seasoned and greatly anointed prayer ministry team. Testimonies of changed lives were abundant. Several from England testified of new life and of freedom from religion they didn't know they had. A man said that when Steve & Kathy came to England, they brought an anointing he had never before experienced. He had been like in a cage with his "heart in by-pass mode". It was not from his heart. "But now I am out of the cage; I am changed." Another young man originally from Wales saw a vision of himself on a hospital gurney headed for the intensive care unit with an ashen, dead look in obvious critical condition. The Lord spoke to him and said, "This is the condition of your spiritual life." God fixed him. He said, "I am now home in the presence of God." He wants to be used to help bring Wales back to its heritage of spiritual revival.

The testimonies of the things God did during these powerful ministry times could fill books. The people from Canada were powerfully touched, especially a group of 50 young people who received an overwhelming touch of God sending them to bring revival to the world. A minister from England preached one service. He spoke the same fresh powerful word of revival and reformation that we have been hearing from Steve Gray in the Smithton Outpouring, only with a full out British accent. His commitment to God and his determination to bring true revival to England was evident. Hundreds of pastors and leaders from twenty-four states were greatly impacted with the reality of true revival, and none of us will ever be the same again.

I have attended all of the pastors and leaders conferences ever held by the Smithton Outpouring, and they have all been powerful and timely. Yet there was an obvious increase in the power and presence of God in this conference. This first conference on the new land, in my opinion, was the first in a season of major increase. Preparation was being made to carry real revival to the world.

CHAPTER 8

A "Typical" Weekend In The Big Tent

Revival continues week after week and year after year, and it continues to increase in spiritual fire at the Smithton Outpouring / World Revival Church in Kansas City. There is no typical weekend. They are all different. The powerful presence of God continues to show up and change hearts, lives, and bodies. God continues to demonstrate His glory in miracles of healing. It is impossible to report all that happens in just one weekend of outpouring services. We can only give you a few typical headlines. The following are from the weekend of outpouring services of November 9-11, 2000. We present here highlights of a somewhat "typical" weekend.

THURSDAY NIGHT

The weekend began with the congregation gathered at the front of the tent, calling out to God to once again come in power this weekend and change us and change the lives of those coming in from across the country and world. We were reaching into the supernatural realm of God, asking desperately for His presence to come down one more time.

Kathy Gray brought a powerful teaching on "People of His Presence". She said, "God has a dream. He is creating a people of authority and anointing to become carriers of His presence." She went on to say that revival is in the people, not in the location. The people make the place holy. Like Abraham, those who wish to be carriers of revival must have faith to follow His presence and leave and go when and where God says. She spoke prophetically, that like the wind, God was loosing us from our roots in the world.

"Keep your shoes on and your passport ready and see how many places you will get your passport stamped. Tonight let's get our passports stamped in prayer. Abraham built an altar when significant things happened, and tonight I want us to build an altar in prayer. An altar is a place of sacrifice and worship. Build your altar tonight; get cleansed from the busyness of the world and the dirt of the day. Abraham believed against all hope. Face facts, but have faith. I am who I am, but God is going to do it. Pick up another stone and build your altar higher." After much more powerful teaching, awesome corporate prayer, worship and high praise led to the ministry time when hundreds received personal prayer ministry and were further prepared and empowered for the powerful outpouring services to come Friday and Saturday nights and Sunday morning.

FRIDAY NIGHT

As the powerful Friday night outpouring service is beginning, people are arriving in the tent while pre-service prayer is again reaching into the heavens, calling for the fire of God to come and consume us. The heavens seem to open wider, and a flow of electrifying power flows upon us as Steve and Kathy come and stand among the people and join in the pre-service prayer. Revival music is loudly pouring forth from the stack of large, black box speakers at both sides of the platform. Yet the music is almost drowned by the roar of the people standing in the area in front of the platform, crying out to God with all their strength. Some praying with hands raised high and arm and body movements speaking body language to God as well as their voices. Some have tears flowing down their cheeks and eyes closed. However, most pour out their petitions with eyes wide open, looking upward toward the heavens as the top of the tent seems to breathe with the prayer force as the tent gently lifts and falls with the night breeze.

As the presence of God begins to move in upon us, some shake and some go to the floor on their knees with their faces near the green turf type carpet as they rock back and forth, and others are motionless in their facedown position. The roar is made up of shouts and moans of intercession and spiritual warfare for tonight's service and for the people coming in. They are crying out to God for the people to be set free and changed. It is a spiritual army at work, loudly engaging in battle with all their strength. Week after week, the effectiveness of this forceful warfare is demonstrated as numerous people are powerfully impacted and changed by the power of God.

The spiritual excitement is now running very high, and great anticipation is filling our hearts as God is again moving among His people of the Outpouring. Many of the guests sit in their chairs, as guests often do, looking somewhat awestruck by what is going on with the regulars in the front of the tent. There is one significant exception to this. A group of guests from El Paso are standing in front of the platform with the regulars, crying out to God with great hunger and desperation for the presence of God to come down.

Eric Nuzum, Kathy Gray, Danny Gray, and the other members of the praise and worship team come to the platform and are now geared up with everything turned on, tuned up, and connected. As usual, there is a great spiritual rush as the glorious live praise and worship for the weekend begins at the Friday service. Our hearts are filled to the bursting point with gratitude, love, and great joy just to be here in the presence of God and experience what He is doing. Sincere praise and worship pour out of our hearts toward heaven as His presence flows in upon us, and our bodies become supercharged with the fire of God. We cannot help but shout praises and sing with the full strength of all our voices as we jump and lift arms in vigorous, vibrant worship and adoration to our awesome God. Truly we feel, as someone has written in a song, better is one day in His house than thousands elsewhere.

The praise and worship continues for much of the evening, mingled with seasons of ministry as the entire body along with the guests are led to give our lives totally to God. Our prayer is verbalized loudly by all in unison as we give our lives completely to Jesus. Pastor Steve has an assistant round up some who have said they wanted to share what God has done for them. Tonight there are several who wish to testify of financial miracles in their lives. Since Pastor Steve and Kathy began several weeks ago to seriously pray individually with people in the services for financial miracles in their lives to provide for the work of the ministry, there have been many amazing testimonies, and tonight is not to be different. Several weeks ago, Steve had asked people to make up their minds, before receiving prayer, what percentage of the increase of miraculous finances they would give to the work of the kingdom. He said, "Be honest with God; make up your mind now whether you will give 100%, 50%, only 10%, or whatever. Then bring your best gift and sow it into the work of the Lord, and we will ask God for the same power that brings healing miracles and restores lives to bring financial miracles into your life. As He answers, you can give more into the work of the kingdom wherever God directs for it to be given."

Pastor Eric Nuzum, our gifted and anointed praise and worship leader at World Revival Church, was anxious to share the financial miracles God had brought forth in his life after sowing a significant gift and receiving prayer several weeks ago. Eric said that in an unprecedented and seldom heard of move, his landlord had come to him and said he wanted to reduce their monthly rent by $60.00 since they were such good tenants and he wanted to give them the month of December free. Then with glowing smile, Eric told of another man who had come to him and said, "I want to cancel the debt of all you owe on your guitar." Eric was hesitant to tell the value of the guitar, but we eventually learned that he had only paid $1500.00 on a guitar worth around $5000.00. Right after this, Eric turned around and opened a shiny, new black guitar case and brought out a new handmade electric guitar worth about $1500.00 and said I've wanted one of these for a long time. On top of everything else, this man said, "I want to give you this guitar free of charge." Wow! Isn't God good? If you knew Eric as I do, you would know these instruments will never be used for anything but bringing forth great honor to God in praise and worship and leading others into His wonderful presence.

A young man wanted to share of the financial increase he had received since Steve prayed with him for financial miracles. He is a young man who has been marvelously transformed by God in revival. To know him now and see his great love for God, his exuberant worship and dedicated sacrificial service, you would never guess that he came to the Smithton Outpouring several years ago with his life in terrible condition. Heavy involvement in drugs, alcohol, and all the perversions and stuff that goes with these addictions had wrecked his life and brought him to deep despair. He met God his first time at the Outpouring and was powerfully changed in a short period of time. He had become a new and different man when he came to Pastor Steve one day several years ago and told him that he needed to be excused from services and from his helper's job for a few weeks. Pastor Steve was a bit taken aback by this wonderful, clean young servant of God's answer to his question as to why. "Well," he said, "Pastor, I hate to tell you, but I have to go to jail for a couple of weeks to settle an old charge against me from my former days." He now has earned a masters degree in economics and serves faithfully and powerfully in the outpouring services.

He said that a few weeks ago he didn't share with the group when, after prayer and sowing his best gift, he received a 12% raise

118

in salary. Since some others were reporting 20%, 30%, and even 40% increases, he felt his insignificant. "But now," he went on to say, "I have received a promotion to a new position in the company where I work, and with the promotion came another 18% pay increase over the 12% a few weeks ago. Now that puts me up there with the rest of them." The crowd enthusiastically applauded with shouts of praise and thanks to God for his testimony.

The flow of revival was evident as one family was leaving to start a church and another was arriving to be changed by revival fire. The family that was leaving came to the platform and shared their good news along with a twinge of sadness. God is sending them out to pioneer a revival church. The family will be moving next month after one and one half years at the Outpouring, during which they were spiritually renewed, rebuilt, and prepared. They said, "We will definitely be coming back and bringing people here to be changed in the powerful presence of God here in this revival."

This was followed by introduction to another pastor and his family just arriving. The new family moved here this week to be renewed in revival fire after years of pastoring a church in Kansas. Pastor Steve asked them to come up on the platform and tell the people a bit about themselves. The wife shakily made it up on the platform and shared, but her nearly seven-foot tall husband never made it up the stairs. He was struck by the power of God and lay in a heap on the steps while She shared a bit about their experience and their desire to be changed in revival.

Praise and worship continue powerfully as the presence of God continues to move upon us. It is the kind of praise that makes you shout for joy to be with Him, and it is the kind of worship that fills your eyes with tears as your heart threatens to burst with love and appreciation for Him. Pastor Steve comes to the keyboard and begins to sing one of the crowd's favorites, "Return To The Lord". As he finishes the heavily anointed song, he asks for only the most desperate and hungry people to come and stand directly in front of the platform. Quickly a number of desperately hungry people run to the front, and soon the altar area is filled with people who appear starving for more of God. Pastor Steve says starving people don't let anything fall from the table; they eat it all. If we are playing in our food, then we are not really hungry and desperate for Him.

I begin to see an awesome vision of a great, golden urn held by two large hands. The hands began to tilt the urn, and liquid fire poures out in a steady stream. I am a bit gone and don't know exactly what Pastor Steve is doing or saying, but suddenly the entire group is powerfully knocked backward and down. The wave of movement begins at the front and center, flowing out in all directions like dominos tumbling down, leaving some people partially upon others. As the power of God sweeps across us and fills our desperate hunger with heavenly bliss—cleansing us, filling us, changing us—He overwhelms our souls and overflows our lives with His wonderful love and presence.

REVIVAL TESTIMONY

Powerful testimonies came forth as a pastor shared excitedly Friday night about how revival fire had spread from Smithton to her church in El Paso, Texas. "My husband and I were called to pioneer our church in El Paso almost nine years ago. My husband was a pastor and a powerful man who did everything well. There wasn't anything in the church that he couldn't do. He had been a rodeo champion, played on a championship football team in 1965, and was a successful blues guitarist and singer. God saved him and called him to preach, and he was a wonderful, kind and gentle man of God. He could play the guitar; he could sing; he could preach; he could teach. He could do it all. My husband was a wonderful man of God and laid a very strong foundation in our church. El Paso is a border town and ministry is hard there. We have seen so many spirit filled churches that just did not make it.

"My husband very suddenly went to be with the Lord January 25th of this year. It totally shocked us. We were not expecting it since my husband was only fifty-five years old. I was rocked; we were all rocked. The Lord made it very clear to me when I was in the ambulance with him that his mantle was passed to me and I was to pastor the church. I really did not see how I could.

"Some friends in California called and said, 'The Grays are going to be here in July, and you must come.' We went. Pastor Kathy had never seen me before in her life. That night, the first night I was there, she came up to me at ministry time and said, "You will live!!!" She told me violently to live and kept praying life over me with great strength. I wanted her to get away from me, because I didn't want to live. I wanted somebody to say, 'You are just going to go and be with your husband.' I wanted to die and not live. I was trying to get her away from me. 'Get her off of me! I don't want to live!' It was at this point that God began a powerful work in my life. I came back from that trip changed.

"As we left, Kathy said, 'Please come to our pastors conference.' I mentioned to a couple of people that we were going. The result of that was thirteen of us came to the pastors conference over Labor Day. Every single one of us who came was noticeably changed. I changed; I experienced the presence of Jesus in a powerful way. We were so noticeably transformed, that when we went back, our people instantly knew we were different. When we had pioneered our church almost nine years ago, we were commissioned by God to be a supernatural church in El Paso. We went back determined that we were going to start to pour out the fresh oil that we received here. We immediately put the band on the stage. We began to do outpouring type prayer and healing prayer. We became a mini Smithton. Praise God! We have had literally supernatural healings.

I Saw The Smithton Outpouring
(Revival On A Small Planet)

People have gone to the doctor, and the doctor has said, 'What did you do? This kind of thing doesn't happen. It must be a miracle, come back in six months, we need to see you again.'

"This time there are thirty of us here! We got an e-mail that spoke of the power of God that hit here September 29th. I told my secretary, 'Call up and see when the Grays are going to be there and book a flight.' So, we booked a flight, just my secretary and I, but the church found out. They said to book a flight for them because they were coming too. So, here we are. We are here, and we want everything that God has for us. We are ready to move forward with revival and the fresh oil. We're allowing the Holy Spirit to pour out in El Paso! We're changed, glory to God!

"We are having opposition. Even my friends in the ministry are like, "Hmmmmm revival? Smithton? Like, Oh!' But we know that this is what we are called to do, and we are doing it. We joined the Revival Network right away because we knew this was the direction that we needed to go. We are literally doing everything that you do here. Before service prayer is like what you have here. We are doing the strong, outpouring type prayer and the healing prayer every service, and we are giving our lives to Jesus every service. We are seeing powerful results. We are seeing new people come every week. They're coming!"

The reality of this testimony was evident in the outpouring services as God visibly, powerfully touched the thirty people. Seemingly, they were right in the center of everything God was doing in these powerful meetings. They were literally swept off their feet on more than one occasion. They were responding to the powerful presence of God with shaking, vibrating, and shouting with joy. And some of them were seen later leaning upon each other and staggering into a local restaurant still heavily under the influence of the Spirit. They will never be the same, and El Paso may just never be the same again either.

A "Typical" Weekend In The Big Tent

FRIDAY NIGHT SERMON

Pastor Steve starts preaching from Matthew 6: verses 31-33.

Mat 6:31-33: So do not worry, saying, 'What shall we eat?' or 'What shall we drink?' or 'What shall we wear?' For the pagans run after all these things, and your heavenly Father knows that you need them. But seek first his kingdom and his righteousness, and all these things will be given to you as well.

Mat 6:7-8: And when you pray, do not keep on babbling like pagans, for they think they will be heard because of their many words. Do not be like them, for your Father knows what you need before you ask him.

"Pagans run after things. Your Father knows what you need. You can live like a pagan and run after things, or you can seek the kingdom of God and things run after you. I am not impressed with things, but I am impressed with how you get things. You can run after things and get some things that way, or you can seek first the kingdom of God and things will be given to you.

"Pagans babble in prayer asking for things. People pray for things they need, and that's what the Father already knows. We know God hears our prayers, and we know if He hears our prayers, He will answer. But the prayers you prayed may not really be called prayer by God, only by you. Prayer that He calls prayer has very little to do with need. Everything we shoot up in the air and call prayer may not really be prayer. Instead of praying first for our needs, Jesus tells us how we should pray in verse nine."

Mat 6:9 "This, then, is how you should pray: 'Our Father in heaven, hallowed be your name."

"Hallowed means honored, respected, and revered. What if my prayer could supply His need instead of seeking my need? There is something that I can supply to God that He doesn't already have. Lucifer's rebellion brought terrible insult and dishonor for God in heaven, His own territory. Throwing Lucifer and all who followed him out of heaven did not completely fix the great dishonor. Similarly, in the earth Satan insulted God, and Adam and Eve went for it and dishonored God. People are yet today dishonoring God on earth.

"What if my prayer can supply something to Him that He needs instead of just seeking my own need? What if we prayed 55 minutes meeting His need and 5 minutes for our need? What can my prayer supply to Him that He will not supply for Himself? What is the one thing that I can supply that He cannot do for Himself? **Honor!** I can give honor to Him with my prayer. I can give Him honor on earth, right in the devil's territory. When we honor Him and restore His honor on earth, the heavens open to us and stay open. We have been put here for a purpose. We have a mission — a reason to sing, to praise, to worship. Our mission is to restore honor to God on earth. Jesus honored God when He refused the devil's offer for the things of this world. It honors God when we don't go after things. Seeking the kingdom of God honors Him."

*Ezekiel 36:22 "Therefore say to the house of Israel, 'This is what the Sovereign LORD says: It is not for your sake, O house of Israel, that I am going to do these things, **but for the sake of My holy name,** which you have profaned among the nations where you have gone.'"*

"Religion has done great damage to the reputation and the name of God by misrepresenting Him as a bad God. God is greatly concerned about His name being honored through His people."

*Ezekiel 36:23 "I will show the holiness of My great name, which has been profaned among the nations, the name you have profaned among them. **Then the nations will know that I am the***

LORD, declares the Sovereign LORD, when I show Myself holy through you before their eyes."

"He will show His name holy in all the earth through you, not because of you. This isn't about you and your name. It is about Him and His name. Religion has sought to teach us that we are special, but since we are all special, then no one is special individually. The word sometimes translated "you" in 2 Cor 6:16 that says "You are the temple of the living God," is plural, not singular. We collectively are the temple of the living God. That does not make us individually special; it makes us a part of something special. Collectively, we are the Bride of Christ. A bride is given great honor. A bride gives much care to be perfect to honor her husband. We are not a bride without things, but a bride that doesn't run after things. Our husband supplies all our needs, and things run after us."

"It is all for His name's sake and has to do with restoring honor to God on earth. Remember the parable in Luke 11:2-13 of the man who has a guest come to his house late in the evening and had no bread for him so he goes to a friend and asks for bread? The passage begins with instruction in prayer. *"He said to them, 'When you pray, say: "Father, hallowed be Your name, Your kingdom come. Give us each day our daily bread.'"* "Hallow the name of God and pray for His kingdom first, and then ask for daily bread."

"The wording in our translation makes it seem that persistence was the reason for the neighbor finally getting up and giving him bread for his guest. But with some understanding of Jewish culture at the time and some study of the Greek wording, the true message becomes clear. In that day, it would have been very shameful to turn away the traveler without bread. The whole community would have been dishonored. If the guest had not received bread, he would have gone elsewhere and would have told the people that they wouldn't give him anything to eat, resulting in shame and dishonor coming upon the entire community. In verse 8, the man will not get out of bed and get the bread because he was a friend, but because of "importunity", he will give him all he needs. Importunity has the meaning of shameless. To prevent shame, he got up and gave the friend the bread. Neither because the man was a friend nor because he was persistent but to prevent shame and dishonor, he gave him the bread he needed."

"We need to be a friend of God, but when you go for bread it won't work. You will not get bread from heaven because you are a friend of God but for the sake of His name. God is restoring His honor, and if you join Him on this mission, He will equip you to fulfill it. If there is something you need to honor Him, just go to Him in prayer and tell Him, 'God, there is something You need to do to prevent more shame from coming upon Your name.' I tell you, He will pop out of bed and give you what you ask."

"These next verses almost seem to be a contradiction as they say all you have to do is ask. But taken in context, the message becomes clear. If an obedient son asks and receives not, does that honor the Father? If he asks for a fish and is given a snake, that would confuse the son and dishonor the Father. Yes, God cares for our needs, but He answers our prayers when we restore honor to Him and His name. It is for His name's sake He answers prayer and sends bread from heaven. God always answers prayer. The problem is that what He calls prayer and what we call prayer may be two different things. What He calls prayer brings honor to His name. What we call prayer may just be sending up our list of wants and needs. Our need for daily bread becomes just a little tag on the end of prayer and worship that honors Him."

SATURDAY NIGHT

Often everything seems to increase on Saturday night. Usually most of the guests have been greatly impacted by the presence of

God and have received one round of powerful prayer ministry and are freer and more ready to receive than the night before. The evening begins with praise and worship starting at a higher level and moving ahead to even greater levels. The big tent is almost filled, and much need is evident in the guests toward the back of the tent. There are many people seeking healing and many in need of serious life adjustments. God moves differently each night. Last night was great rejoicing and great pouring out of His Spirit. Other times are relaxed and sometimes sweet as gentle waves of love flow over us. But tonight is to be a work night for sure, and God has brought out the powerful heavy-duty machinery. The presence of God is rolling like big, roaring tractors blowing diesel smoke and ready to bring great change. The powerful winds are blowing like standing to close to the highway when the big trucks roar by at seventy miles per hour. The prayer warriors have their work cut out for them tonight, but they are more than ready, fully empowered and ready to attack the enemy and do away with his works. The praise music roars with power of the Spirit and seems to be driven by the engine of the drums.

After waves of powerful praise and worship, people are called to the front to receive healing prayer. Soon the front looks like a battle field with people strewn all about as Steve & Kathy reach out to take the hands of the rows of people and speak healing into their bodies and they fall to the floor or are seemingly knocked backward. A few remain standing like pillars, seemingly untouched by the power of God all around them. Some will not receive, but others who seemed to not receive will find later that what used to be a problem isn't there anymore. There are more people coming for prayer than can fit in the front of the tent, so the ushers form a line down the center aisle of people seeking prayer. Steve & Kathy will go down the aisle and pray for them last. When some in the front get up and return to their seats, others are moved up into the vacated space to be prayed for.

No one knows how many are healed of various ailments, and the service moves on while some are yet on the floor. But there are always some who testify on the spot of instant healing. Others will write or call later and tell of what God did for them tonight after they return to their doctors for confirmation. We no longer need to count healings to validate what God is doing; it is very obvious how powerfully He is moving among us. Neither do we try to count those who make commitment to God as there are far too many to keep up with anyway.

Pastor Steve preaches from John 3. Find ways to honor God, and remove things that dishonor Him. Do the honorable thing...praise and worship Him and live righteously.

1 John 3:7: "Dear children, do not let anyone lead you astray. He who does what is right is righteous, just as He is righteous."

"If we say we are God's, then we should do right. We have, for years, lied in church as we stood and sang 'I Surrender All' over and over again and did not do it. If we say it and it is untrue, it is a lie. We need to do it or come up with a new song like, 'Don't Expect It All' or 'I Surrender A Couple of Things'. We become false prophets, saying what is untrue. False prophets come in sheep's clothing, not shepherds' gear. We may be all bent out of shape about some preacher, trying to prove he is a false prophet, but the wolf comes in sheep's clothing.

"The love of Jesus destroys the work of the enemy. The righteousness of God works righteousness in you. Some think Jesus came just to give us a hug and get us to heaven. This undermines doing anything in this life. Jesus came to destroy the work of the devil. Love destroys the work of the enemy. We must restore honor to His name by destroying the devil's work. To leave people tied up when we have the power to change the situation is not love and does not honor God.

"Remember the Canaanite women who came to Jesus on behalf of her daughter who was demon possessed? Jesus told her that it was not right to take the children's bread and toss it to the dogs. This woman knew what was going on in Israel. They were allowing the gifts of God to fall to the floor. When people allow gifts to fall to the floor, someone else can pick them up. Israel, for the most part, was not receiving Jesus and the bread that He brought. They did not take Him seriously as the Messiah. In a sense, they were playing in their food and allowing pieces of bread to fall from the table. If we are playing in our food, it is because we are not really hungry. This Canaanite woman was seriously hungry and picked up the bread falling from Israel's table and her daughter was delivered.

"We must win the love battle to destroy the works of the devil. *1 John 3:10-13: 'This is how we know who the children of God are and who the children of the devil are: Anyone who does not do what is right is not a child of God; nor is anyone who does not love his brother. This is the message you heard from the beginning: We should love one another. Do not be like Cain, who belonged to the evil one and murdered his brother. **And why did he murder him? Because his own actions were evil and his brother's were righteous.** Do not be surprised, my brothers, if the world hates you.'*

"Cain lost the love battle. He hated his brother because his brother did what was right. He became evil because of righteousness in his brother. If we win the love battle, we win the murder battle. If we are not righteous and do not have love for our brother, when real righteousness comes upon the scene, evil becomes infuriated. The dormant stuff down inside shows up when true apostles show up. When real revival comes, those who were well enough but didn't have love will become angry and rise up in the spirit of Cain with murder in their heart for their brother."

SUNDAY MORNING

Sunday morning services are generally just the same as Outpouring Services on Friday and Saturday nights. The praise and worship and excitement are the same. The crowd is usually a bit smaller because many of the out of town guests have left to return to their home churches, but there are others from the local area visiting the services as well as some of the out of town guests. Overall, there is a little more emphasis on the local congregation because largely it is the church body that is present. Sunday morning is a good time for Tom & Diana Trout to take care of any church business and inform the group of church activities. It is also a good time to hear testimonies from some of the church members on what God is doing in their lives.

One couple gave testimony in the Sunday morning service about their recent South East Asia trip with the Grays. The wife spoke first, "We had the privilege of going on a team to Japan and Singapore. It's a privilege to go and to give honor to the Lord and to our pastors. We have gone with Pastor Steve & Kathy before. More and more, I see that they are willing to pour their lives out for the lives of others. They plead with the people; they go to any lengths. They sacrifice anything for the lives of others, and all of you are a part of what they are doing.

"Just an example of how you people play a part in this. A couple of months ago, A man from Singapore came here. Church, you touched him. Back home at his church in Singapore, his pastor was frustrated and ready to quit the ministry, but this man brought back revival to the his home church because he saw it in you. When he came here, his life was changed. We met Him at the conference in Singapore. He came with his pastor and a group of about thirty people from their church. During the conference in Singapore, I worked the book table at the back and wasn't up front. There was

130

reconciliation between representatives of two major denominations. As the leaders from both churches stood in the front reconciling, I was straining to hear, but I felt the waves back at that book table. That is the heart of the Lord -- reconciliation, of people, of denominations.

"You heard testimony Friday night about what is happening between a Word church and the World Revival Church. This revival is going all over the world, and you guys are a part of it. When people come here, they see fire. You are carriers of fire, vessels that are willing to be broken and used, and look at what has happened. Who knows where it is going to go from here. Paul said, 'Follow my example.' My pastors say, 'Follow my example,' and I am going to follow their example whatever it takes."

The husband spoke next, "We had a great time. What an honor to be able to follow our pastors. I would have never been able to go to Japan or Singapore, but because of Pastor Steve and Kathy, those doors that are wide open to them were open to us. They are so gracious to let others come along. I was allowed to walk through that door with them and to minister to people on the other side of the world. I could have never done that myself. There is no way! I just thank and honor our pastors for allowing us to go with them and be a part of the ministry there. Lives were changed.

"There is nothing more heartwarming than to go into a conference and see people who are stiff and stuck changed by the power of God. People all over the world are the same; they are stuck in religion. They are stuck in the world and stuck on themselves. There is absolutely no difference in the spiritual needs around the world. They have different skin colors and cultures, but the problems are the same wherever you go. That's why revival is needed all over the world. There is nothing greater than to see our pastor go in like the master surgeon. The first thing he does is give them anesthesia. He comes in and pours out his love and compassion and just gives his heart to them so they know that he loves and cares for them. Then when he pulls out the spiritual scalpel and begins to cut and the Holy Spirit begins to convict and to reveal, they are not full of anger, but they are so thankful and so grateful.

"We were in Malaysia ,and I have never been treated so well in my life. The people were so hungry, so longing for more. We were in Japan and Singapore, and leaders of both conferences said that they never have the same speaker back twice. Yet both of them want to have Pastor Steve and Kathy back. When the power of God came in, and they knew a man of God had come in, they just cast all their rules aside. Unfortunately, the sad part is that there are so few true men of God who come to them. I just encourage you to lift Pastor Steve and Kathy up in prayer and support them however you can. We did five or six services a day while on the trip. Pastor Steve would go one way, and Kathy would go another way and preach. People just wanted more and more of what God was flowing through them."

A couple who are students in the World Revival School of Ministry and very much a part of revival, gave testimony of how God brought them to Kansas City. The wife spoke first. "The Lord has been drawing us here for a long time. I have been coming to outpouring services here from time to time for the last couple of years. People were always giving testimonies of how God was pulling them there. I said, 'Lord take us there. Bring us here. I want to go there so badly. The Lord is there, and people are hungry for God. That's my heart and where I need to be.'

"Last year while we were living in Rockford, God started pulling us even more strongly towards revival. We had some revival up there, but not like this. In April, my husband's business sold. He kind of started another small business. We didn't know the school was happening at that time. He came home and told me that he had gotten an e-mail that there was a school. In my heart, the spirit just leaped inside of me. I wanted to go. I said, 'Oh, that's nice.' I didn't want to influence my husband in any way. It had to be God. I don't want to do anything just because I want to do it. I want to be led by the Spirit every step. He was kind of doing the same thing.

"We prayed about it, and we came down here and spent a weekend. The Lord did a work in our hearts. He said, 'It is going to cost you everything,' but I said, 'It is worth it.' When we die to ourselves, He just brings us life. Just coming down here to the front for prayer last night was so powerful and life changing. Last night after prayer, I was just thinking, 'Lord, thank you so much.' I just thank Him so much that I get to be here. It is such an honor— such an honor to serve the Lord."

The husband spoke next, "He led me to sell my business, and I did that. There is a whole long story behind it, too long to tell just now. We got down here, and I was patting myself on the back saying, 'Man, you really sacrificed for the Lord.' Then I found out that was normal here. You all pack up and leave and go where God tells you to — you just do it. What's been happening to me this past three months since I have been in school is that God has systematically disassembled me and laid me on the floor. What that has done to me is helped get rid of all the junk and garbage. My life is just totally changed and rearranged. The only thing I want to do is serve Him. I was asked this morning where God was leading, and I said that I don't know and I don't care any more. It's up to Him. He can do with me whatever He pleases. This is such a restful state of mind to be in. I have anticipation, but it's not for me to do something, but just to bring honor to His name."

SUNDAY MORNING SERMON

Sometimes on Sunday morning, especially after Steve and Kathy have been on the road ministering somewhere else on Monday through Wednesday and return to Kansas City in time to preach Friday night and Saturday night in the outpouring services, Kathy will preach the Sunday morning message. However, this week Steve also preached Sunday morning. His message remained on the same theme as earlier in the week, but it became a bit more specific toward some of the needs of the church people. He spoke from 1 Corinthians, and I must admit that as the conviction began to come upon me at the end of the message, I felt that the pastor might be speaking specifically to me. I even sent a communication later to ask if he had me in mind. Of course, I always felt guilty as a child. When the teacher would clamp down on the class about something that someone had done, I felt and looked so guilty that the teacher often thought I was the guilty party.

1 Cor 1:26-29: "Brothers, think of what you were when you were called. Not many of you were wise by human standards; not many were influential; not many were of noble birth. But God chose the foolish things of the world to shame the wise; God chose the weak things of the world to shame the strong. He chose the lowly things of this world and the despised things—and the things that are not—to nullify the things that are, so that no one may boast before him."

Pastor Steve pointed out that most of us who have been called to serve God here in the revival were called when we were nobodies because we were nobodies. "Now some of you have become know-it-alls and argue. You did not know enough to argue about things when you were called. Some study diligently and take many careful notes but for the wrong reasons. It is all so they can have their own glorious ministry someday. Some increase in natural human wisdom, and human wisdom empties the cross of its power. You were called when we were nothing, and now you want to be something. Some of you may need to return to the humble state of mind when God first called you."

Chapter 8
A "Typical" Weekend In The Big Tent

The prayer ministry team came forward for the last ministry time of the week. The out of town guests who remain come along with much of the congregation for one more blast of the Spirit and one more time of receiving prayer ministry. After an hour or so of ministry time, the floor is only spotted with bodies as many have gotten up and are moving on to begin their trip back home or are headed for their favorite restaurant to get a bite to eat and reflect on the weekend.

CHAPTER 9

Miracles Continue In The Big Tent

The outpouring of God did not let up after the powerful pastors conference. People from Australia, England and Canada were at the next regular Friday night outpouring service. Powerful praise and worship led into a public prayer to receive Jesus and give our lives to Him as the crowd roared their acceptance and commitment.

BAPTIZED IN THE SPIRIT

Pastor Steve Gray was led to bring about another "first" for the Smithton Outpouring. In the past, those seeking the baptism of the Holy Spirit received ministry at the end of the service during regular prayer ministry. This Friday and Saturday night, he called for those who wanted to receive the baptism of the Holy Spirit to come forward. Over thirty people, ranging from children to older adults, came to the front and were soon joyously praising God in heavenly languages.

MANY HEALED

Pastor Steve briefly instructed the people in receiving healing to "Take your medicine from heaven." A strong anointing came as the altars filled with people seeking healing as Steve & Kathy prayed for them. People fell quickly and powerfully to the floor as they were touched by the power of God. Several testified after the healing prayer.

A young woman testified from her motorized wheelchair of miraculous healing. She is a full-size saint of God with a vibrant spirit and joyous soul in a very tiny body with obvious birth defects. Her vivacious voice filled the tent with life as she testified of emotional healing since coming to the Outpouring over two months ago. She had previously gone to a Bible college and had to leave. She felt she had left her life purpose and was very discouraged. She had a lung disorder and had to be on a breathing machine two or three times each day. The next day after prayer, her lungs suddenly opened up, and she has not been on the breathing machine for two months.

An eleven-year-old boy, said he had a hearing deficit of 10 decibels, and he often had to ask his mom and others to repeat what they had said. He went on to say that he received prayer last week, and his hearing was healed. He admitted that he was too shy to testify, so he used the excuse of needing to get verification. He had a hearing test the next week that confirmed that he had no hearing deficit.

Testimonies were given of many marvelous healings from heads to toes. One man said he had dropped a 50-pound weight on his foot at work, breaking his toe, and he was instantly healed tonight. A young man testified of receiving prayer last week for diabetes. Previously he had been taking insulin shots twice a day, but he had taken only one shot since getting prayer for healing because he didn't need them.

LIVES HEALED

Several testified, as hundreds could have, of changed lives. One man in his twenties said he had been in the Smithton Community Church for years growing up. He went to college and taught himself to be a self-made man. As a result, his life hit bottom, and he was aware of the devil laughing at him after deceiving him and wrecking his life. After everything he had done for himself crashed, he decided to come back to revival. For weeks, he put on a happy face when he came to church but cried in brokenness at home. With a big smile, he said, "But now God is putting my life back together. He is changing my life again."

A young teenage boy said, "I have battled pride and depression and kept coming for prayer. Last night He touched me." With tears he testified, "He has changed me — no more depression. I will serve Him with my whole life forever."

A teenage girl wants to reach teens at her school, but her efforts have not been well received. She came for prayer last night, and the prayer warrior prayed for her "crown of self government" to be removed. She said, "I had never before known that I was a self-willed controller. I asked my parents and others, and they confirmed my need. That prayer and that phrase 'crown of self government' have changed my life. When you crown yourself, you crown yourself big and wonderful, but all that crown does is weigh you down. I didn't know it was in me, but now it is gone."

SPONTANEOUS POWERFUL MINISTRY

It was late Saturday night after a powerful ministry session, and most of the guests had received prayer and left. The prayer warriors and ministry team yet remained, ministering primarily to one another. We were suddenly aware of an excitement similar to a tornado in the Spirit. Kathy Gray moved out onto the ministry area and began to pray violently for the people. As she approached a line of six to eight intercessors and reached her hand out toward them, they all suddenly shook violently and fell to the floor. Kathy moved about the room in great power, and people fell like they were mowed down with automatic weapons as she prayed blessing and protection over them.

Miracles Continue In The Big Tent

OUTPOURING MOVES TO A NEW LEVEL

Once in a while, God does something so extraordinary that words can't describe what He has done. Friday night, September 29, 2000 was one of those times that God came down and moved the Outpouring to a new level. I can only relate this to the spiritual lightning strike that sparked the Outpouring over four years earlier. However, this lightning that struck September 29th, hit the entire church body and many of the visitors. Everyone was so powerfully struck that I could not take notes. I was too overcome by the power of God to observe the move of God.

The unprecedented move of God began as Pastor Steve Gray stepped to the platform after a season of great worship and praise. He spoke with awesome anointing and great authority. From his first words, the power of God struck us. There was no introduction or lead into it. The power of God just struck us instantly and powerfully as Pastor Steve spoke directly into our hearts, challenging us to a higher place with God. He spoke of our being chosen to stand in the gap for many and asked have we been faithful to pray with our whole heart, worship with all we are, and praise with all we have. People began to crumple to the floor in tears, and moaning and groaning of deep, agonizing repentance filled the tent as many knelt or hid our faces in the carpet, under the awesome presence of God moving upon us. I have no words to describe the glory and the agony, the fear and the ecstasy, as His awesome presence broke and elated our hearts.

Suddenly the need of the people of the world came into our focus. More clearly than ever, we heard the commission of God to give up everything of this life, to do and to become the people of God who will fulfill His purpose in the earth. Our needs and frustrations became nothing, and God's desires became our everything.

Pastor Steve continued under the supernatural anointing with awesome power in every word as he called for only those of the Outpouring who would admit that they had been doing something less than praying, worshiping, praising, and serving with their whole heart. He asked them not to just come forward for prayer, but only if they truly wanted to repent and be changed. The whole front of the church filled instantly with hundreds of desperate people, including many who have been a part of the Outpouring for years. We were not to be restrained or denied because nothing mattered but the presence of God and getting ourselves emptied before Him.

Visiting pastors were powerfully ministered to as the presence of God filled the tent in response to a powerful roar of prayer from the people. Pastor Steve & Kathy stepped forward and laid hands on the pastors while Eric led the people in worship. After our hearts were rent, our souls emptied, and our very lives wrung out before God, Steve & Kathy began to pray powerfully for the people of the Outpouring and spoke the awesome increase of God's powerful presence into our lives. Tissue boxes were long ago emptied, and all pride, self-focus or self-concern had left us. Now the great increase filled us, and some people fell as dead, some violently shook, and at least one lady was frozen in place. There were many obvious responses as the powerful increase poured into us. God has moved this outpouring to a new level in one night. In one service, everything has been turned up and can never be the same again. Pastor Steve then moved directly to the preaching of the Word although it was difficult for him to speak in the heavy presence of God.

There is no doubt that God was preparing us to move on to a greater level of world ministry. The sense of transition was great as we were being changed and empowered even more by His presence. The time in the tent was transition time and development time for a new, world-focused ministry.

CHAPTER 10

World Ministry Develops

WORLD REVIVAL SCHOOL OF MINISTRY

People must be trained and prepared to carry revival to the world. The World Revival School of Ministry began classes on September 11, 2000. A pastor of a church in the area graciously offered the use of their facilities so the school could begin, rather than wait for a building to be built. Students began receiving personal training, practical experience, and impartation of the Spirit as well as Biblical knowledge. They began learning from proven revival ministers and participating first hand in the Smithton Outpouring. The two-year program was designed to be a mix of courses in revival history, theology, spiritual development and preaching, combined with practical revival ministry experience to equip and empower the student to be effective in revival on the ministry field. Evening classes were also offered for those who could not attend day classes.

Pastor Steve Gray, school founder, said, "Our objective is to have a training center that will teach men and women how to impart revival to the local church, how to maintain it themselves, and how to pioneer churches with the foundation of revival, as well as train students in Scripture and prepare them for ministry."

WRSM EXPLODED INTO BEING

God's presence and participation was evident in the powerful, soul-stirring dedication of school faculty and students Sunday morning, September 10, 2000 in the big tent at the World Revival Church. Pastor Steve Gray told the group of students gathered at the front of the church that, "We are not calling you to learn. We are calling you to live, and a part of living is learning." He went on to say, "When you get to where you are going, they don't want to know what you know. They want to know how to live. You are getting an education so you can take life." "WE GIVE YOU LIFE NOW — TAKE IT!" At that moment, the entire group was struck by the power of God and instantly fell to the floor. a mass of lifeless-looking bodies receiving life from God. I was again impacted with the destiny of this work of God, preparing sold out, Christ-centered men and women to carry the reality of the Spirit of God across the world, bringing revival and reformation to the church and world.

World Revival School of Ministry began classes with more students than expected and has grown every trimester since its inception. Experienced school people had advised that the goal of starting a new school on such short notice was impossible, but when God is in a thing, nothing is impossible. We believe He definitely has a timely purpose for this school.

God had sent a doctor of theology to become the school administrator. He had slipped into the Smithton Outpouring services unannounced some time ago in search of more of God and the experience of revival in his own life. No one at Smithton knew of his training, abilities, and potential until the need arose. He became Academic Dean of WRSM. He has 14 years pastoral experience and 8 years teaching experience at the university and Bible college level. He holds a THD in Pastoral Theology from Faith Bible College & Theological Seminary and an MA in Historical Theology from Oral Roberts University and was greatly impacted by revival at Smithton.

GOD'S PROVISION OF PEOPLE FOR TRANSITION

The school administrator is one example of how God has from the beginning raised up or sent people to fill the many positions of service and leadership required by this expanding ministry. The period of time in the tent was a time of transition. The ministry was transitioning from the Smithton Outpouring in a small town to the World Revival Church in Kansas City with a much greater world focus. Everything was being multiplied. Many new works and needs presented themselves. One major need to help touch the world was a powerful web site and e-mail distribution of news and information to inform thousands across the nation and around the world of what God was doing in Kansas City.

God drew a talented man and his family to become part of the revival. He is a very accomplished graphic artist with much experience in designing quality web sites, and he is a devout Christian. He was seeking more of God and an experience with real revival when he came to Smithton, and he arrived just in time to be available to design powerful and quality web sites for World Revival Church and for World Revival Network of Ministries and Churches. He also plays drums for the praise and worship team, and both he and his wife are enrolled in the World Revival School of Ministry. Their entire family, even their children, are actively involved in every outpouring service at WRC.

Barbara and I felt a great drawing to move to Smithton just at the time of the move to Kansas City. I had experience in writing and e-mail ministry and distribution. We arrived just at the right time to help begin the Outpouring Times E-mail Newsletter, a semi-monthly publication sent to thousands around the world.

An accomplished journalist who had experience with major Christian magazines, arrived at Smithton seeking revival. She was on hand at the right time to head up many areas of publications and media presentations, including radio and TV.

Another woman heard the call to Smithton through reading a Charisma magazine article. She had experience in running TV cameras in a church and arrived just in time to set up the new TV cameras and coordinate and train operators for the TV ministry. These examples could go on as God has sent many talented and prepared people to carry out the work of spreading the fire of revival and the word of the kingdom to Kansas City and the world.

INCREASE OF REVIVAL FLAMES TOUCH THE WORLD

As the power and presence of God increased in the big tent, the outreach ministry was increasing in intensity and breadth as well. The Smithton Outpouring was touching people and churches from the east coast to the west coast in the USA, South East Asia, England, and many other parts of the world with revival fire.

REVIVAL TOUCHES EASTERN USA

From North Carolina up to Maine, the power and presence of God from the Midwest was flowing to the east. The same outpouring that had brought a stream of 250,000 people from across the nation and sixty foreign countries to Smithton, Missouri and now Kansas City was flowing into churches in the eastern USA. Pastor Steve & Kathy Gray and Pastor Dan & Shelly Gray from the Smithton Outpouring, in several separate meetings over several weeks, were spreading the fire of the Smithton Outpouring revival in the East Coast region of our nation.

Care Pastor Danny Gray is Senior Pastor Steve Gray's brother. Though they minister in very different styles, they both bring the same powerful message of reformation and revival from the Smithton Outpouring. Their anointed preaching cuts right through all our excuses and misconceptions of who we really are, and why we can't give our all to God, and why we can't experience a powerful move of God.

Chapter 10
World Ministry Develops

Pastor Steve Gray flowed back and forth across the platform at a church in North Carolina as around eight hundred people hung on every word. He moved so by the Spirit that power seemed to smoothly flow from every movement, every gesture, and every word. The anointing was so strong and our hearts so prepared that the words seemed to flow directly into our hearts, touching every thing within us and creating a great hunger for God in our lives. Each word stirred a greater hunger for purity and holiness, a desire to lay down everything and be filled with His life. Our lives seemed tainted and soiled by even the best parts of our ways of doing and being. Our hearts wept as we understood how we had sought after many things of church and life but had not made room for a mighty move of God.

Even seasoned ministers who were not strangers to the work of God found themselves getting free of man's religion and worldliness that they didn't realize they had as their lives were suddenly exposed to themselves in the presence of the all mighty, all innocent, and all glorious God. The Spirit and presence of God brought forth the real meaning of Scriptures we had heard for years as revelation flowed in context from the Word. It is as if our hearts were opened, and all the covering to our souls pulled away, and we could see that we had filled our lives with many good things, and perhaps a few secret things, and had not made room for a true move of God. We must make room for a move of God and allow Him to consume our lives to bring forth an outpouring that will change our families, our churches, our cities, and eventually our world.

No longer were we thinking what could God do for me today — what blessing can I receive. Our hearts were crying out, "God, what do you want me to do for You? How can I bless You? Here I am. Tell me what You want, and I will do it." Our souls had melted, and our spirits cried out for more of Him, to give more of ourselves to Him. Our lives can never be the same again, and we must be with Him, and we must let others know of His awesome beauty and glory. We didn't need the wonderful miracles of healing and manifestations to prove or to know His love. Yet, the healings flowed, and the miracles came in His presence, and lives were forever changed.

REVIVAL TOUCHES SOUTH EAST ASIA

In a nation where Islam is the official religion, hundreds of church leaders from many denominations flooded the altars desperate for a touch from God after hearing Pastor Steve Gray preach the word of the kingdom with power. With tears streaming down their faces, many of these leaders collapsed to the floor, trembling and weeping as they experienced the fire and glorious visitation of the Lord for the first time. Church leaders in Kuala Lumpur, Malaysia's capital, said they felt fire sweep over their bodies when Pastor Steve prayed for the fire of revival to touch them. Leaders from Singapore, Malaysia, and Indonesia gathered at several conferences to capture the fire of revival and the Word of the Kingdom that has blazed in Missouri for over five years. The conferences in Singapore and Malaysia were characterized by ministries and leaders instantly transformed when exposed to the glory of the Lord. At a conference sponsored by a major denomination, officials said the gathering was historic because it was the first time other denominations attended, the attendance record was broken, and a reconciliation took place between two conflicting denominations. In Kuala Lumpur, church leaders had to turn away visitors at evening Outpouring Services where over 1,000 people crammed into one of the largest Charismatic churches in Malaysia.

Pastor Steve and Kathy poured apostolically into these church leaders who are hungry for a move of God. From the first morning of services in Kuala Lumpur, Pastor Steve's fiery preaching aroused a hunger for a move of God among the people. "What if the presence of God was more real than the music, place or people?" He asked the audience that held onto every word. "This is why the apostles could preach under the threat of persecution. The presence of God is more real than the presence of man." The message pierced hearts sending hundreds forward to the altar for prayer. One lady was delivered from demons when Kathy Gray prayed for her. As the woman rolled on the floor screaming, Kathy took authority, and Jesus set the woman free. The next day, she came to the meeting transformed and healed of the debilitating disease of fibromyalgia.

At the conference, the fire of revival tore down walls between two denominations. The Outpouring changed a major denominational church when two of its members attended services at the World Revival Church in Kansas City.

When they returned to their homeland, their leaders wanted to receive the revival that they had experienced. Within a week, the leaders brought a group of 30 families with them to the conference.

We made an apology, and we forgave them," said one of the denomoninational leaders of Singapore. "Pastor Steve prayed for our reconciliation, and we see that revival breaks down walls." Not only does revival break down walls between denominations, but in relationships. "When my husband came to the Outpouring in Kansas City, he came back a different man," said the wife of one of the men. "God healed my marriage, and this is why I came to the summit."

At the summit, Pastor Steve's powerful preaching and the intense prayer ministry changed leaders. "I didn't know how distant I was from God until I heard Pastor Steve's preaching," said a worship pastor of one of the largest churches in Singapore. During the last service, Pastor Steve prophetically challenged the leaders to be willing to abandon their prosperity to touch the harvest. "We don't

147

know what's on the horizon. Everything could change in a day," he said. "Would you be willing to give up your prosperity and your comfort for the sake of a harvest? Jesus is bringing a revival that will turn into your survival." For the first time, church leaders in Singapore and Malaysia realized they have to be changed by revival to reach the great harvest in their countries.

During a recent ministry trip to Japan, God moved upon church leaders there as Pastor Steve Gray poured out revival fire of the Smithton Outpouring anointing to them. The scene of hundreds of church leaders flooding the altars with tears streaming down their faces, collapsing and trembling under the Glory of God has been common during the ministry of Pastor Steve Gray. "Many churches, pastors and believers were touched by the sparks of revival," says the pastor of one of the churches in Kyushu, Japan. "I strongly believe that the Lord is about to visit this land of Japan, and now is our time to prepare the way of the Lord."

Over 80 churches from many denominations were represented at the Pastors and Leaders conference in Kyushu, Japan. Prior to the conference in Kyushu, Pastor Gray was the keynote speaker at a conference in Tokyo. In the meetings, Gray says he came with a prepared sermon, but the Spirit of God overruled him as he pastored the leaders into revival. During one of the meetings, over 500 people gathered on the stage desperate for a touch from God. They all collapsed under the glory of the Lord that entered the room. Despite preaching through an interpreter, the message that came through was fresh. "I preached messages that I had never preached before, or even thought of," he says.

Revival is also transforming ministries in the Philippines. A Philippino man said, "In 1999 a group of 11 church leaders from the Philippines came to the Smithton Outpouring in search of revival," "God touched them and set them on fire with revival. Now the fire is burning in the Philippines. They had heard of other revivals, but after hearing of the Smithton Outpouring, decided to make the long journey to the Missouri cornfields in their quest for more of God."

Since that visit, he says that teenagers are being changed by revival. At a recent worship concert, the glory of the Lord came down, and he watched 2,000 people on the basketball court fall under the power of the Holy Spirit. "Every day of the week, our youth and singles gather to pray for the revival of our nation," he says. "I believe that prayer moves heaven. I learned that from Pastor Steve Gray, and I believe that prayer moving heaven is already moving the Philippines into revival."

With the flares of revival being stirred in Japan, Malaysia, Singapore, and the Philippines, God has set the stage for a move of God in Southeast Asia that could change the face of Christianity around the world.

TIME IN THE BIG TENT ENDS

The giant air conditioners had pumped all the cold air they could through the large black tubes and kept the tent reasonably comfortable in the summer heat. A covering of large blue plastic tarpaulins had been added on top of the tent to help retain some of the air conditioning. Even in the extra hot summer days of 110F degrees heat, meetings went on comfortably in the big blue-and-orange-striped tent with the blue plastic shield on top. Some of the evening meetings were even a bit too cool as the ushers struggled to manage the temperature control.

The new building that some builders had told us would take two years to build was coming along rapidly, and we all had hoped that by some miracle we would be able to get into it before really cold winter weather came. This was not to be, and large propane tanks were brought in and connected to the large air conditioning and heating units, and the big strange looking black tubes began to pump heat into the tent. The weather seemed to change almost instantly from extreme heat to bitter cold. December was the coldest ever on record in Kansas City. The bitter cold came in wave after wave without warm-ups in between. Propane delivery trucks made regular trips to fill our large and rapidly drained tanks; however, it was unbelievably comfortable in the tent. Of course, a sweater felt good especially if you were seated very close to the thin side curtain that was the only separation between the warm inside and the bitter cold outside. Even in the bitter cold and snow and ice, there was always a good crowd of regulars and at least some visitors for every service. Although, I am sure there were many people who just could not handle coming out in the bitter cold to have church in a tent.

The transition time from the Smithton Outpouring to World Revival Church was drawing to a close. The building miraculously was coming to a sufficient level of completion that we could soon move the services into it. The day and night work of committed workers who sacrificed everything to push the construction ahead and miraculous intervention bringing favor with city officials and government agencies had done what could not be done. We were able to move into the large foyer to hold services while the huge sanctuary was being made ready. I am not sure anyone understood the great changes that were occurring and the significance of the changes that were before us. The Smithton Outpouring ended and became the foundation of the much greater anointing of the World Revival Church. This only became obvious to some of us as the move was made into the new building. The increases of the past months of transition began to be better understood in light of the vast new thing God began in World Revival Church.

CHAPTER 11

World Revival Church

The awesome services in the big tent had been wonderful, but fresh history was to be made as the Outpouring moved into our new building on Friday night, January 5, 2001. As the move was made, there were changes in name and in the spiritual realm, as "The Smithton Outpouring" became "The World Revival Church" in name, definition, and anointing. The world-size anointing began to settle upon the church. Hearts and visions began to expand, and the reality of touching the world began to come into focus. Faith and ideas began to be planted into the minds and hearts of the people and the leadership of the World Revival Church.

Services were held in the foyer of the bright new building while the rest of the building was being completed. Pastor Steve's first message in the new building, on "Christ in You, the Hope of Glory", established the foundation in a new phase of the Outpouring. The message sharpened the focus to the hope of glory as the object of our faith. God's glory doesn't come from outer space, but from Christ in us. We have two problems according to *Romans 3:23: "For all have sinned and — fall short of the glory of God."* We can repent of our sin but yet not have the glory of God. The term "fall short" sounds as though we almost made it, but this scripture actually states that we lack the glory of God. The hope of that glory, pouring into us, and then back out of us, is what keeps this revival going.

Friday night was good, but Saturday night the powerful presence of God really moved in. It began when the doors were opened to the line of people waiting outside. They quickly filled the foyer, which is larger than the whole building was in Smithton. Kathy Gray encouraged the tightly packed crowd of people gathering at the front of the church in powerful pre-service prayer. Praise was awesome as the people cried out to God for His presence and revival fire to come. Worship deepened as a surge of people rushed forward toward the platform and fell to their knees and upon their faces in the presence of God. Our hearts melted as we again experienced the awesome, loving presence of God that is beyond all we could ask or think. Pastor Steve's message focused on *Mat. 22:21 "Give to Caesar what is Caesar's, and to God what is God's."* The great revolutionary revival message is not, as the Jewish people then supposed, to not pay taxes and revolt against Rome. The really revolutionary message for them and for the church today is to **give to God what belongs to Him**. We belong to Him, and truly giving ourselves to Him is the message of revival.

Sunday morning the sense of destiny was stronger than ever before. Memories of the old Smithton Community Church came to mind as people from the Kansas City area and at least ten states were packed in, filling the large foyer and spilling over into an overflow room. Kathy Gray brought a powerful and very significant message defining World Revival Church and our mission. "We are called to carry revival to the world," she said. Kathy defined the church as called out ones, who are called together as sons of light dispelling darkness. Specifically, God has called people of all ages to this church from Canada, North Carolina, and all across the nation, people who have sold their homes and moved to Kansas City to become carriers of revival. She defined revival as life returning to God's people as the people return to their first love, which involves repentance and brings refreshing. She defined the world as the people who live in our neighborhood and work next to us, then the communities and cities and the nations. We are called to carry revival to the world, and our vision is to touch the world using methods and ideas old and new with the breath of God on them. A strategy is developing within the leadership of World Revival Church to touch the world by using new ideas and redeeming old ideas, methods, and plans with the spirit of revival. We are products of the past works of God and the sacrifices of those who have gone before us with the roots of this outpouring going back 100 years in this very area.

100 YEARS OF PENTECOST IN KANSAS CITY

It would be difficult to believe there is no significance in the fact that exactly one hundred years ago to the day in this same area the modern Pentecostal Revival began. One hundred years ago, January 1, 1901, the move of God that became the world wide Pentecostal revival of today began in Topeka, Kansas, less than 70 miles from the permanent location of the World Revival Church / Smithton Outpouring and moved into Kansas City a few days later.

You may have heard a lot about Azusa and perhaps William Seymour, but have you heard of Agnes M. Ozman? It was January 1st, 1901, the first day of the new century, when Agnes M. Ozman became the first known person in recent history to be baptized with the Holy Ghost with the initial evidence of speaking in other tongues. As Charles Fox Parham prayed for her and laid hands on her, she was baptized in the Holy Spirit, and the experience of the baptism of the Holy Spirit was restored to the Body of Christ. This began what has become the greatest move of God in modern times. Charles Fox Parham had previously founded the Bethel Bible School in Topeka, which became the 20th century birthing place of the outpouring of the Spirit in the United States. Within a year, Brother Parham and other students were also baptized in the Holy Spirit. Brother Parham closed the school and began to conduct revival meetings throughout the Midwest.

In December of 1905, Parham opened a Bible Training School at 503 Rusk Street in Houston, Texas, and by 1907, 13,000 people had passed through the school. One of those people was a 31-year-old black man named William Joseph Seymour. Due to strong segregation and blatant racism in the church at that time, Seymour was not allowed to sit in the classroom and listened through an open door as he sat in another room.

Seymour moved on to Los Angeles where he and others were baptized in the Holy Spirit at meetings in the home of Richard and Ruth Asbery at 216 North Bonnie Brae Street. From there, the group moved to 312 Azusa Street where the mighty Outpouring of the Holy Spirit occurred that has now matured and spread to the world. Now, 100 years later, from the same heartland area of Kansas City USA, the powerful Smithton Outpouring is pouring out to the World through the World Revival Church. It seems more than a coincidence that the World Revival Church moved into the large new building on the 62 acres of land in Kansas City exactly 100 years from the beginning of the Outpouring at Bethel Bible School, which was just down the road in Topeka, Kansas. The Outpouring of today is much matured from the early beginnings of a century ago. At World Revival Church, the powerful miracles and manifestations of the Holy Spirit are accompanied by powerful reformation preaching of the Word of the Kingdom much like Jesus preached 2,000 years ago.

God is making a new thing, a new and fresh outpouring of His Spirit to establish a new work with a greater mission and a stronger impact. The World Revival Church is being defined and established as a new thing beyond the Smithton Outpouring of the past. As wonderful as the old was, the new is greater. The message is the same but more piercing and more powerfully flowing to peoples and churches around the world. The vision is the same but greatly enlarged and enhanced with increased reality of the Spirit and the Word of God.

The Smithton Outpouring was the beginning of a major avenue for the flow of the fire of God bringing a new level of purity and devotion to Christ. The church in general around the world has begun to move toward more reality of commitment and loyalty to Jesus, replacing lukewarm religion. This is not a new thing to God; it is His design for His Bride that has been from the beginning.

The new anointing for World Revival Church is greater than the Smithton Outpouring of the past and is here in awesome demonstrations of His power and strong cutting, piercing, life-changing word from God. God's historical pattern is to start a new season or a new thing with glorious demonstrations of His presence and power. At the birth of Christ, He sent angels in the heavens, and at Pentecost, He sent a rushing mighty wind and tongues of fire. Those of us who missed the exciting powerful presence of the first days of the Smithton Outpouring in 1996 have had a second opportunity to experience the glorious days of beginning fire at the World Revival Church 2001outpouring. Spectacular weekends of mountaintop highs of exuberant praise and unrestrained joy in the Holy Spirit came forth at World Revival Church as longing and desperation met His loving presence in the early weeks in the new building. Steve and Kathy wrote of this time, "World Revival Church is in a season of explosive increase and new beginning. People who have been with us in revival for a long time said that the power of God is more explosive now than in recent years. Some said it is a new beginning similar to the initial outpouring. At a recent service, people were immediately impacted as our prayer warriors stepped toward the masses that were seeking prayer ministry. The power of God was so strong that several of the seasoned prayer warriors were overcome themselves. We believe that God is turning up the fire to prepare us for the explosive increase of revival that is upon us."

I Saw The Smithton Outpouring
(Revival On A Small Planet)

FROM THE FOYER INTO THE BIG NEW SANCTUARY

For the first time since the beginning of the revival, there was plenty of room for wide aisles and moving about. We were only seeing a portion of the entire sanctuary, but it seemed so large and the ceiling so high. Again a sense of future destiny came upon many who rejoiced at what God had done and was going to do. It was not hard to envision the building completely filled with those seeking revival. There was a temporary wall behind the temporary platform that was about fifty feet in front of where the permanent platform was to be built. The temporary wall only went up part way toward the high ceiling, and large sheets of black plastic completed the wall to the top of the ceiling. The floor was not yet carpeted, revealing concrete spotted with paint, and the side walls were not yet covered with sheet rock, but the place was beautiful to us as we entered and felt the presence of God. The smell of fresh paint and other building materials was present, but it was no distraction to most of the worshipers.

The chairs were still the folding kind from the tent, and some of them dated back to the beginning years in the gymnasium/revival hall at Smithton. The huge familiar black box speakers were stacked on either side of the platform and would be turned up loud to fill the large room with sound. A large section of temporary carpet was laid down in front of the platform to make it a little softer for people who fell while receiving prayer ministry, but the carpet was never big enough for weekend outpouring services, meaning that many always wound up lying on the concrete. Catchers were careful to try not to bounce any heads, but it was hard on clothing. Especially those who wore something dark would often get up later with white chalky spots on their clothes, but revival people don't care as long as the presence of God is there and lives are being

156

changed. After all, it was much warmer than being in the tent. It was exciting to come in week after week to new changes as the construction process continued around us.

The presence of God was as powerful as a mighty wind at times when heavenly fire fell, and at other times, it was as sweet as honey and as gentle as a spring breeze. On Friday night, February 9, 2001, we once again got a taste of the honey of the land as the Holy Spirit moved with sweetness in our midst. In the middle of praise and worship, Pastor Steve Gray called out a member of World Revival Church and brought him to the front. He asked the man what he wanted from God, and after a few minutes of silence, he only asked to go to the Holy of Holies. As simply and gently as a father, Pastor Steve told him, "Just go." With that simple request and those simple words, a golden river of sweetness began to flow from the throne of God.

Slowly, more people began to move toward the front of the church. One by one people eased their way to the altar area, like those unable to hurry their way across a river of honey. Soon the altar and aisles were filled with men, women, and children, each determined to go into a new place with God. Tears filled the eyes of many as longing for the Lord churned in their hearts.

Pastor Steve wove his way through the hungry and hopeful, praying for each one. He began telling people that they had asked a good thing, but an easy thing. "You know the way; just go there. Go to Him," he gently urged. As the heartfelt prayers of a body of people touched the heart of God, He filled the room with His gentle presence. After all the prayers were spoken, a river of praise, gratitude, and awe flowed back to the Lord. Yet even then, God had more richness for specific individuals as Pastor Kathy Gray began flowing with the Spirit and singing prophetically to several members of WRC. These words from God fell like golden drops of honey on the lips, allowing people to taste even more of the goodness of the Lord.

By the end of praise and worship, the single river of honey diverged into countless streams of the sweetness of the presence of God. In those holy moments when time stood still, our faithful God once again led a group of His people into a land flowing with milk and   honey.
The sweetness became fire at the altar at the next weekend outpouring services. On Saturday, February 17, 2001, the fire of God fell upon the altar of World Revival Church, and the congregation rushed to its purifying flame. Through five years of revival, most of the members of the church have learned to respond quickly to the stirrings of the Holy Spirit in the midst of a service, so they scrambled to the front almost as one body when the fire of God began to fall. They swarmed the front of the church and filled much of the center aisle in their eagerness to be in the middle of whatever God wanted to do.

Passionate, heartfelt songs rose to heaven, crying out for the God Who is an all-consuming fire. The fire that fell met good kindling and ignited a raging inferno. All over the church, people experienced a literal burning feeling as they drew near the flames. One woman's head and neck felt very hot and turned red, and another woman received healing from severe lower back pain as heat burned down her back. Entire blocks of people were knocked from their feet as the power of the Holy Spirit swept through their midst. Far from seeking protection from the flames, all ages were putting themselves in the best position to be totally consumed by the transforming fire of God.

Later in the evening, another bundle of wood caught flame, but it probably went unrecognized by many. After all, a campfire might burn intensely, but it will go unnoticed next to a forest fire.

As prayer time wound down, a couple of the kids from the youth group suggested that they all needed to get together on the side of the ministry area and pray. The entire group ended up on their faces on the floor, some completely prostrate, weeping in repentance of living far short of the glory of God. They stayed a very long time in this position of repentance, asking for the entire group to be set ablaze. The church was basically empty by the time they rose to their feet again, but their hearts were full of the fire of the Lord and passion for Him.

Seeking a clear definition of revival will bring an incredible number of different responses. Yet, no matter what people call it, God is clearly on the move when the lives of children and teens are being radically transformed.

REVIVAL LEADERS VISIT THE OUTPOURING

In the summer of 2000, Rodney Howard-Brown and Mike Bickle had ministered to the outpouring at a major meeting hosted by the World Revival Network in Kansas City. Dr. Robert White, former General Overseer of the Church of God, Cleveland, TN., was the first leader to visit in 2001 after the move into the new building. He spoke to pastors and leaders at a World Revival Network meeting in February 2001. The meeting attracted hundreds of leaders from around the country to Kansas City. Dr. White said, "The Holy Spirit spoke to me about Pastor Steve and Kathy in such a way that has only happened three times before." He added that with the people, technology, resources and power of God flowing, there was potential to impact the world with a Holy Ghost revival, but the Body of Christ was fragmented. "Steve Gray could be catalyst or the fuse the Holy Ghost can light in order to bring the Body of Christ, especially the Pentecostal/Charismatic sector, together in a common effort that would ignite America in revival." Dr. White has ministered over 40 years. He and his wife, Kathy, visited with a staff member of World Revival Church after a leaders' meeting in the afternoon and gave the following interview.

Question: Dr. White, what do you see happening with revival in America?

Answer: I believe America is ripe for revival and there is a real hunger wherever I go from the people. Churches and individuals are hungry for God. Churches that are having revival are growing. The people are hungry, but denominational and Charismatic leaders are not assuming responsibility of doing anything about revival. They want to stay in the comfort zone. Most denominations work within the parameters of what's acceptable in that group.

Question: What sets apart Pastor Steve Gray?

Answer: What sets him apart is that he does not try to lift himself up. There's humility about him, and he wants to lift up Christ. There is no evidence of him trying to promote himself. God is looking for someone who will give Him all the glory. Pastor Steve has all the credentials, and what's unique about his ministry is that he can identify with the average church. 50 percent of the Pentecostal Churches are status quo, 25 percent of the churches are dying and 25 percent are growing and thriving. Pastor Steve comes along to the 50 percent that may want to quit and gives a message of what God can do for them.

Steve can identify with the wounded and hurting pastor in small towns and villages because God gave him a revival in a small town of 532. If God will give a revival in a cornfield attracting thousands of people from all over the world, then He can give a revival to that small town or small church where most of our pastors labor.

Pastor Steve and Kathy are willing to look beyond their own fellowship and denomination to bring the body of Christ together.

Question: What do you see on the horizon with revival?

Answer: God is always doing something different. The Smithton Outpouring created a hunger in people who are use to cold, dry dead services. The Outpouring brought them to the fire and let them get warm, and now they have to have the same fire in their church. God has His own signature on the revivals at Brownsville, Toronto, and the Smithton Outpouring. **I believe God has raised up Pastor Steve and Kathy Gray to give leadership to revival.**

Pastor John Kilpatrick from the Brownsville Revival in Pensacola, Florida was the next revival leader to visit the World Revival church in the new building. He came in March 2001 to be a part of the Smithton Revival anniversary celebration.

5-YEAR ANNIVERSARY OF THE SMITHTON OUTPOURING

March 24, 2001 was the fifth anniversary of the fire of God that ignited the outpouring of revival. It was fitting that Pastor John Kilpatrick of the Brownsville Revival at Pensacola was the guest speaker at the anniversary celebration attended by around 1000 people Friday evening. It was a little over five years ago that Pastor Steve Gray visited the Brownsville Revival in Pensacola incognito, and his hope of revival in his own life and the Smithton Community Church was restored. The celebration along with the dedication of the new building took place in the spacious but yet not fully completed 25,000-sq. ft. building on its beautiful 62-acre campus.

In an historical moment, Pastor John Kilpatrick presented two plaques, one to Steve Gray and one to Kathy Gray, honoring them for their five years of leadership in the Smithton Outpouring revival that is now touching the world as World Revival Church.

Pastor John Kilpatrick spoke on moving on to the next level. He said that the devil could see when God was about to pour out a great blessing and would attack viciously to attempt to steal the blessing. He spoke from his own personal experience of hearing the enemy say on three different occasions that he was going to destroy him and his ministry and then hearing God say " No, I am going to bless you." In each case, severe personal attacks upon himself and his ministry were endured before awesome blessing and phenomenal growth took place. He said the key is to stay in place and keep going. He finished the message by speaking a great blessing coming upon Pastor Steve and Kathy Gray and the ministry of World Revival Church.

Mike Bickle spoke briefly on breaking out to break through and reiterated the blessing he had spoken last summer on Steve & Kathy Gray and the World Revival Church. He said he was glad when he heard the Smithton Outpouring was coming to Kansas City and that the churches in Kansas City would be better because of the Smithton Outpouring being here.

Charisma Magazine and Remnant Magazine as well as Channel 4 TV were on hand to cover the event. The celebration ended Sunday afternoon with a release of 1000 balloons, many with valuable prize coupons attached along with personal invitations to visit the World Revival Church. Pastor Steve said, "We want to let the people of Kansas City know that we are here and they are welcome here."

NEW BEGINNING AFTER 5 YEARS

Today is a day in the season of major shift — of massive change at World Revival Church — truly a day of movement to a new and greater level. There are many changes in walking with God. Every weekend at World Revival Church is like turning a new blank page of a book. Every weekend, new things are written in our book of life, and we don't know what they will be until they come forth. We do however know that they will fit in general with the preceding weekend. Then, once in a while, a greater shift occurs which is like a whole new chapter is begun. There is a greater shift as we change to a whole new chapter of life with God. This shift — this major change today — is more than a new chapter. I believe the Lord showed it to me as closing the book. He is closing the book and handing us another fresh new book. It is a new beginning and not just a new chapter, but also a whole new book.The old book was wonderful. The 5th anniversary services at World Revival Church on Friday and Saturday nights, March 23 and 24th, 2001 were a look back. It was wonderful when Pastor Steve & Kathy were honored with beautiful plaques from revival leader John Kilpatrick of the Brownsville Revival in Pensacola for their five years of leading the Smithton Outpouring Revival. When our pastors are honored, all of us who have served with them are honored. Yet as wonderful as that honor for the past is, today begins a whole new book, and our eyes move to this day and the future — the next five years and more. World Revival Church is being positioned by God to reach out to the world and bring change. The shift is much larger than just World Revival Church. A new season of God is upon the world. The season of the man-centered church emphasis age is ending, and the glorious kingdom emphasis age is begining.

These changes at WRC became evident around the first of this year. In January, the church moved into the new building. The day of the move into the new building was almost one hundred years ago to the day from the last major shift of God in the world. Just down the road in Topeka, Kansas, the new Pentecostal movement began one hundred years ago and quickly came to Kansas City. It spread to Texas and then to Azusa Street in California. In the last 100 years, the Pentecostal revival has spread to the entire world. The prophecy of Joel Chapter 2 came about as the Holy Spirit was poured out, and sons and daughters prophesied, and young men saw visions, and old men dreamed dreams.

Now, in this new kingdom emphasis age, GOD IS RAISING UP A MIGHTY ARMY to bring a different kind of war. A war beyond deliverance and healing — a mighty army bringing purity, devotion to Christ, holiness, loyalty, honesty, true commitment to God, restoring honor to God in our world.

Joel 3:9-12: Proclaim this among the nations: "Prepare for war! Wake up the mighty men, Let all the men of war draw near, Let them come up. Beat your plowshares into swords And your pruning hooks into spears; Let the weak say, 'I am strong.'" Assemble and come, all you nations, And gather together all around. Cause Your mighty ones to go down there, O LORD. Let the nations be wakened.

Those of us who have been walking with God for many years sometimes forget how things are in the world. It has been a long time since I lived an empty, useless life without meaning or purpose. A life of following my own sick heart, a life of selfish pleasure that soon was not even fun but a bondage of a multitude of filthy addictions and evil striving is far behind me. I forget that the children of the world have been sold out for pleasure. The lukewarm, man-centered church has allowed corruption to steal the children of the world and take them into captivity. God is raising up an army of pure and powerful warriors to take back what has been stolen.

Joel 3:1-3: For behold, in those days and at that time, When I bring back the captives of Judah and Jerusalem, I will also gather all nations, And bring them down to the Valley of Jehoshaphat; And I will enter into judgment with them there On account of My people, My heritage Israel, Whom they have scattered among the nations; They have also divided up My land. They have cast lots

World Revival Church

for My people, Have given a boy as payment for a harlot, And sold a girl for wine, that they may drink.

We at World Revival Church are a part of the army that is much more that just WRC, but is made up of many leaders and many troops around the world. We must take our next step. As Pastor Steve & Kathy Gray lead us, we must move forward and take our next step as the army of God. There needs to be many men and women who are revival leaders bringing forth the fire of revival and the word of the kingdom around the world.

All revival people around the world need to be ready to step ahead to our next level of service. All pastors, praise and worship people, prayer warriors, intercessors, staff members, teachers, ushers, car parkers, helps and every worshiper, worker, and minister must move ahead with God as revival increases in our world. We are not talking about elevation of position. We are all just drops of water in the river of God. We are talking about rising to the occasion of becoming faithful servants in the war of Christ to redeem the kingdom.

This is the time for World Revival Church and revival churches around the world to receive anointing and become an army to change the world. This is the time to be filled with compassion for the world and passion for our God. As Pastor Steve recently said, "It is time to be filled and to be spilled." Steve pointed out that five years ago on March 24, 1996 he was preaching "you must be filled" and on March 24, 2001 he was preaching, "You must be spilled." On both occasions, he used the Scripture of the woman pouring out the alabaster box of precious ointment. Some scoffers said, "What a waste!" Just as some scoffers of revival today look at revival people pouring out their precious lives instead of going after the pleasures and things of the world and say, "What a waste!" But Jesus said the woman would be spoken of forever and that what she had done was in preparation for His burial, and yet His crucifixion was not yet. We are a part now of preparing the way of the Lord and His imminent glory.

Destiny is in the air, and most everyone feels the significance of the revival coming forth in our world and our part in it at World Revival Church. A student at World Revival School of Ministry, said it well when she wrote in a report about the anniversary weekend, "Smithton Community Church is now an amazing memory, and World Revival Church is headed to a new place, a higher level in preparation of the way of the Lord. We will be the John the Baptist Generation!"

This unending story is far from finished. Though the Smithton Outpouring is past, the World Revival Church and the awesome revival spawned by the Smithton Outpouring has only begun. The world waits as all creation moans in thirst and hunger for the pure-hearted, devoted, loyal soldiers birthed in the Smithton Outpouring and other outpourings around the world to bring the glory of God. World revival, establishing the ways of the kingdom of God, is within sight as the fire of revival and the Word of the kingdom are preached and demonstrated in power by an army of innocent, pure-hearted soldiers who are as wise as serpents but as harmless as doves. And of His kingdom there shall be no end.